The Duty of
Self-Denial

and Ten Other Sermons

Thomas Watson

Soli Deo Gloria Publications
. . . for instruction in righteousness . . .

Soli Deo Gloria Publications
An imprint of Reformation Heritage Books
2965 Leonard St. NE
Grand Rapids, MI 49525
616-977-0889
orders@heritagebooks.org
www.heritagebooks.org

Paperback reprint 2021

ISBN 978-1-60178-824-5

The Duty of Self-Denial was first published in 1675. Seven of the ten other sermons were taken from *Sermons on Several Subjects Preached by Mr. Thomas Watson* (London, 1689). Grateful acknowledgement is given to the Evangelical Library in London for the loan of this book. The remaining three sermons were taken from the six-volume set *The Morning Exercises at Cripplegate* (London: James Nichols, 1844).

For additional Reformed literature, request a free book list from Reformation Heritage Books at the above regular or email address.

Contents

The
Duty
of
Self-Denial

by
Thomas Watson
Minister of the Gospel

To the Reader

Christian Reader,

The weightiness of the argument here discoursed on justly merits a larger volume. But I have contracted it because it may possibly come into more hands. I must profess I do not know a more necessary point in divinity. Self-denial is the first principle of Christianity. It is the life-blood which must run through the whole body of religion. Self-denial is learned not out of the topics of philosophy but the oracles of Scripture.

It is my request to the reader to peruse this manual with seriousness, knowing that the practice of self-denial is that wherein his salvation is nearly concerned. May the Lord work with His Word and cause the dew of His blessing to fall with this manna, which is the prayer of,

Thy Friend and Servant in the Gospel,
Thomas Watson
Dowgate, 1675

Chapter 1

"And He said to them all, If any man will come after Me, let him deny himself." Luke 9:23

*A Preliminary Discourse Wherein the
Proposition Is Comprised*

"All Scripture is given by inspiration of God, and is profitable for doctrine," 2 Timothy 3:16. The Word is compared to a lamp for its illuminating quality, Psalm 119:105, and to refined silver for its enriching quality, Psalm 12:6. Among other parts of sacred writ, this is not the least: "If any man will come after Me, let him deny himself."

These words are dropped from the lips of Christ, the oracle of truth. In the preceding verse, our blessed Savior foretold His passion: "The Son of Man must suffer many things." And His suffering is set down in two expressions:

1. He must be rejected. Thus He was the "stone which the builders refused," Psalm 118:22.

2. He must be slain. This diamond must be cut. He who gave life to others must Himself die. And as Christ thus abased Himself for us, so we must deny ourselves for Him. "And He said to them all, If any man will come after Me, let him deny himself." Self-denial is the foundation of godliness, and if this is not well laid, all

3

the building will fall. Let me explain the words:
1. "And He said to them all." Self-denial is of universal extent. It concerns all; it respects both ministers and people. Christ spoke it as well to His apostles as to the rest of His hearers.
2. "If any man will come after Me." If he will follow Me as the soldier does his general, if he will arrive at that place of glory where I am going.
3. "Let him deny himself." Beza and Erasmus render it, "Let him lay aside or reject himself." Self-denial is a kind of self-annihilation. The words have two parts:
First, a supposal: "If any man will come after Me."
Second, an imposal: "Let him deny himself." This word "let him deny" is not only a permission but an injunction. It carries in it the force of a command. It is as if a king should say, "Let it be enacted."
The proposition I shall insist on is that a good Christian must be a self-denier. "Let him deny himself."

Chapter 2

The Explaining of the Proposition

QUESTION 1. In what sense must a Christian *not* deny himself?

RESPONSE 1. He must not deny his promise. A man's promise should be sacred. He is to keep it though it is to his loss, Psalm 15:1,4. He who makes no reckoning of his promise, God makes no reckoning of his profession.

RESPONSE 2. A Christian must not deny his grace. He must not disown any good work wrought in him. He ought not to say that he is a dry tree when the dew of heaven lies upon his branches. As it is a sin for a man to make himself better than he is, so it is to make himself worse. To say he has grace when he has none is presumption. To say he has no grace when he has is ingratitude. It is bearing false witness against the Spirit of God.

QUESTION 2. In what sense must a Christian deny himself?

RESPONSE. I answer in general that he must deny that carnal part which is near to him as himself, that which is the apple of his eye. But more particularly:

1. A Christian must deny his reason. I do not say renounce it, but deny it. Some cry up the Diana of reason, making it the rule and standard of faith. Indeed,

5

that there is a God and that this God is to be worshipped is a law written in the heart of man and is con-
sonant to reason. But who God is and the right mode
of worship is such an arcane matter that reason can no
more find out than the Philistines could Samson's riddle. Job 11:7: "Canst thou by searching find out God?"
    Reason must be denied in *credendis* and in *agendis*.
    In *credendis*, that is, in doctrines proposed to be be-
lieved:
    The doctrine of the Trinity. The well is deep, and who
can with the plumbline of reason fathom it! The persons in the Trinity are distinguished but not divided.
They are three subsistences but one essence. The
Trinity is purely an object of faith. There are some
truths in religion demonstrable by reason, such as that
we should flee vice and do to others as we would have
them do to us. But the Trinity of persons in the unity
of essence is of divine revelation and must be assented
to by faith. Those illuminated philosophers who could
discourse subtlely of the magnitude and influence of
the stars, the nature of plants and minerals, could not
by their deepest investigation find out the mystery of
the Trinity. This is wholly supernatural and must be
adored with humble believing.
    The doctrine of the Incarnation. This is the doctrine
that eternity should be born, that He who rules the
stars should suck the breasts, that a virgin should con-
ceive, that the branch should bear the root, that in
Christ there should be two natures yet but one person,
that the divine nature should not be translated into the
human, yet the human nature should be assumed into
the person of the Son of God, the human nature not
God yet one with God; here reason must be denied.

The doctrine of the Resurrection. That the body interred, nay, crumbled into a thousand factions and the ashes scattered in the air, should rise again is above reason to imagine. The Epicureans and Stoics derided Paul when he preached to them of the resurrection, Acts 17:22. Here reason must be taken captive, John 5:28. "Marvel not at this, for the hour is coming in which all that are in the graves shall hear His voice and shall come forth," 1 Corinthians 15:42-43. The chemist can, out of several means mingled together, extract the one from the other, the silver from the gold, the alchemy from the silver, and can reduce every metal to its own species. So, when the bodies of men are mixed with other substances, the wise God can make a sudden extraction and clothe every soul with its own body. Did not the same particular body rise, it would be rather a creation than a resurrection. Acts 26:8: "Why should it be thought incredible that God should raise the dead?" God can do it because of His power, Matthew 22:29. And He cannot *but* do it because of His truth.

The doctrines of faith do not oppose reason but transcend it.

Reason must be denied in *agendis,* that is, in duties enjoined to be practiced. There are many duties in religion which carnal reason quarrels at. God said, "It is the glory of a man to pass by an offense," Proverbs 19:11.

No, says carnal reason, it is cowardice. The heathens thought it gallantry of spirit to avenge injuries.

God says that the paths of holiness are strewn with roses. Proverbs 3:17: "Her ways are ways of pleasantness."

No, says reason, they are severe and cynical. I must
crucify my delights and drown my mirth in tears.

God says that religion is gainful. 1 Timothy 6:8:
"Godliness is great gain." It brings contentment arising
from the favor of God. It brings temporal riches.
Proverbs 3:16: "In her left hand riches and honor."
The way to be prosperous is to be pious.

No, says reason, if I follow the trade of religion I
shall break. 2 Chronicles 25:9: "What shall I do for the
hundred talents?" In this case, carnal reason must be
denied and fought against. He who will go no farther
than reason will come many leagues short of heaven.

2. A Christian must deny his will. This is Brugensis'
gloss upon the text: "The will is the great wheel in the
soul that moves all the affections." The will in innocence was regular. It echoed God's will. But since the
fall, though it retains its freedom in moral actions, yet
spiritually it is depraved. If the will could cease from
sinning, said Bernard, there would be no hell. The
greatest wound is fallen upon the will. The mariner's
compass, being stricken with thunder, causes the point
of the needle to be wrong. Man's nature being cor-
rupted causes the will to point wrong; it points to evil.
There is in the will not only impotence but obstinancy.
Acts 7:51: "Ye have always resisted the Holy Ghost."

Here we must deny our will and bring it to God's
will. If a crooked stick is laid upon ground that is level,
we do not try to bring the ground even with the stick,
but to make the stick even with the ground. So God's
will is not to be brought to ours, but our will being
crooked must be brought to God's will. We pray, "Thy
will be done." The way to have our will is to deny it.

3. A Christian must deny his own righteousness, his civilities, duties, and good works. Philippians 3:9: "That I may be found in Him not having mine own righteousness." The spider weaves a web out of her own bowels. A hypocrite would spin a web of salvation out of his own righteousness. But St. Paul, like the bee, sucked salvation from the flower of Christ's righteousness. Isaiah 64:6: "Our righteousnesses are as filthy rags." Our best duties are fly-blown with sin. Put gold in the fire and there comes out dross. Our most golden services are mixed with unbelief. The angel pouring sweet odors into the prayers of the saints, Revelation 8:3, shows that they are in themselves unsavory and need Christ's sweet odors to perfume them.

Use duty, but trust Christ's righteousness for salvation. Noah's dove made use of her wings to fly but trusted the ark for safety.

And, if we must deny our holy things in point of justification, then much more our civilities. A stake may be finely painted, but it has no root. A man may be painted with civility and yet have no root of grace. A moral person is washed, not changed. The life may be civil when the heart is wicked just as the sea may be calm when the water is salty. The Pharisee could say he was no adulterer, Luke 18:11, but he could not say he was not proud.

The civilized person may have a secret antipathy against goodness. He may hate grace as much as vice. Civility is but a cracked title to heaven. A piece of brass may shine, but, lacking the king's image, it will not pass as currency. A man may shine with moral virtues, but lacking the image of God consisting in holiness he will not pass as currency at the day of judgment.

Morality is good, but God will say, "Yet thou lackest one thing," Mark 10:31. Civility is a good Jacob's staff to walk with among men, but it is a bad Jacob's ladder to climb up to heaven.

4. A Christian must deny all self-confidence. How confident was Pendleton of himself! "This fat of mine shall melt in the fire of Christ," he said [Foxe's *Acts and Monuments*], but instead of that his courage melted. The same Hebrew word signifies both confidence and folly. Self-confidence betrays folly. Peter presumed too much on his own strength, Matthew 26:34: "Though I should die with Thee, yet will I not deny Thee." But how soon was his confidence shaken and blown down with the breath of a maid? Matthew 26:71-72: "He denied with an oath, saying, I know not the man." Peter's denying of Christ was for lack of denying himself. Self-jealousy is good. Romans 11:20: "Be not high-minded, but fear." The trembling reed often stands when the confident cedar falls. Who that knows the fierceness of a trial or the falseness of his heart will not fear? How have some professors shined like stars in the church's hemisphere yet have been falling stars? Porphyry, Julian, Cardinal Pool, Gardner, Judas. The Apostles have been called by some of the ancients "the eyes of the world," Christ's feet, the church's breasts. Judas was one of these, yet a traitor.

Nay, some of the saints, through God's withdrawing the influence of His Spirit, have relapsed for a time, such as Cranmer and Origen, whose heart fainted in the seventh persecution and he offered incense to the idol.

Deny self-confidence. 1 Corinthians 10:12: "Let him

that thinketh he standeth take heed lest he fall." 'Tis just with God that he who trusts himself should be left to himself. The vine being weak twists about the elm to support it. A good Christian, being conscious of his own imbecility, twists by faith about Christ. Philippians 4:13: "I can do all things through Christ's strengthening me." Samson's strength lay in his hair. Ours lies in our head, Christ.

5. A Christian must deny self-conceit. Job 11:12: "Vain man would be wise." In the Hebrew it is "empty man." Man is a proud piece of flesh. He is apt to have a high opinion of himself. Acts 8:9: "There was a certain man named Simon, giving out that himself was some great one." Sapor calls himself "Brother of the Sun and Moon." Commodus the Emperor called himself "The Golden Hercules." The Persian kings had their images worshipped by all who came into Babylon. Such as view themselves in the flattering glass of self-love appear bigger in their own eyes than they are. They think their spark is a sun, their drop a sea. They are highly conceited of their acumen, their wit and parts, and are ready to despise others. The Chinese say that Europe has one eye and they have two, and all the rest of the world is blind.

Deny self-conceit. Romans 12:3: "I say to every man that is among you, not to think of himself more highly than he ought to think." Proverbs 23:4: "Cease from thy own wisdom." It does not say cease from *being* wise, but from *thinking* yourself wise, Proverbs 3:7 and Philippians 2:3.

That you may deny all high, supercilious thoughts of yourselves, consider:

Self-conceit is no small sin. Chrysostom calls it the mother of hell. It is a kind of idolatry, a self-worshipping.

Whatever noble endowment you have is borrowed. As the man said of the axe which fell in the water, 2 Kings 6:5, "Alas, master, for it was borrowed." All a man's gifts, his pregnancy of parts and ripeness of wit, are borrowed from heaven. And what wise man would be proud of a jewel that was lent to him? 1 Corinthians 4:7: "What has thou that thou didst not receive?" The moon has no cause to be conceited of her light for which she is beholden to the sun.

Whatever acuteness of wit or sageness of judgment you have, think how far short you come.

How far short do you come of that knowledge which Adam had in innocence? He was the oracle of wisdom. He could unlock nature's dark cabinet and find out those secrets which amuse us. Adam had a full inspection into the causes of things. He was a kind of earthly angel.

But how far short do you come of him? Your knowledge is checkered with ignorance. There are many hard knots in nature which cannot be easily untied, like why the loadstone should draw iron and leave gold and pearl, or why the Nile should overflow in the summer when waters are usually lowest. Job 38:24: "What way is the light parted?" Why is the sea higher than the earth and yet does not drown it? How do the bones grow in the womb? Ecclesiastes 11:5. What is the reason of all occult qualities? He who sees clearest has a mist before his eyes. By eating of the tree of knowledge, we lost the key of knowledge.

How far short do you come of that knowledge

Satan has? He is call "demon" from his knowledge. We read of "the depths of Satan," Revelation 2:24, and his stratagems, 2 Corinthians 2:11. Satan is an intelligent spirit. Though he has lost his sanctity, yet not his knowledge. Though he has lost his breastplate, yet not his headpiece. He has wit enough to deceive the nations, Revelation 20:3. His understanding is nimble, and, being compared with ours, is like the swift flight of an eagle compared with the slow motion of a snail. Why, then, should any be puffed up with conceit of their knowledge wherein the devil far outstrips them?

How far short do you come of the knowledge they have who are perfected in glory? He who is higher than a dwarf may be lower than a giant. Such as excel others in natural abilities are of a lower stature than the glorified saints. 1 Corinthians 13:12: "We see through a glass darkly." But the saints in bliss have a full-eyed vision of God. Their light which burned here like fire when it is smothered is now blown up into a pure flame. An infant glorified knows more than the most profound rabbis on earth. In heaven, all shadows fly away, the sun of righteousness having risen there with his illustrious beams. This may pull down the plumes of pride and self-conceit.

Your dark side is broader than your light side. Your ignorance is more than your knowledge. Your knowledge is but as the light of a torch, your ignorance as the Cimmerian darkness. Job 26:14: "How little a portion is known of God?" The Septuagint renders it, "How little a drop!" To think to comprehend the Deity is as if we should go to span the ocean. Christians, the greatest part of your knowledge is not as much as the least part of your ignorance. This may demolish all high imaginations. You have no cause to be conceited of the knowledge you have, but rather to be humbled for what you lack.

Think what a hell of sin you carry about you. Sin is the accursed thing, Joshua 5:13. It is the quintessence of evil. It is like a stain to beauty. It was typified by the menstrual cloth, which was the most unclean thing under the Law. Though you have knowledge, sin eclipses it. It is as if a woman should have a fair face but a cancer in her breast. You knowledge does not so much adorn you as sin debases you.

Grace can never thrive where self-conceit grows. As a body cannot thrive in a dropsy, so neither can the soul thrive which is swelled with this dropsy of pride and self-conceit. A proud head makes a barren heart.

A supercilious conceitedness is odious, and much lessens any worth in a person. 'Tis like a cloud in a diamond. The more one values himself, the less God and angels value him. Let a person be eminent, yet, if he is self-conceited, he is loved by none. He is like a physician who has the plague. Though he may be admired for his skill, yet none care to come near him.

Such as have a high opinion of their own excellencies are on the ready way to ruin. Either God infatuates them, Isaiah 29:14, or denies a blessing to their labors, or suffers them to fall into some great sin. Peter, who was so well-conceited of himself, as if he had more grace than all the Apostles besides, the Lord let him fall very far. He denied Christ with an oath, nay, an imprecation, Matthew 26:74. Peter wished a curse on himself if he knew Christ; nay, some think he cursed Christ.

The Lord sometimes lets vain, conceited persons

fall not only foully but finally. The doves, said Pliny, take pride in their feathers, and in their flying high at last they soar so high that they are a prey to the hawk. So, when men fly high in self-conceitedness, they become a prey to the prince of the air. Let all this make us deny ourselves; let it kill the worm of self-conceit. If we are proud of our knowledge, the devil does not care how much we know. Let St. Paul be our pattern. Though he was the chief of the Apostles, he calls himself the least of saints, Ephesians 3:8 and 2 Corinthians 12:11. "Though I be nothing." This illustrious Apostle, a star of the first magnitude, shrank into nothing in his own eyes. 'Tis excellent to be like Moses, whose face had a luster on it, but "he wist not that the skin of his face did shine," Exodus 34:29.

6. A Christian must deny his appetite. The sensitive appetite is sick of a bulimia; it cries, "Give, give," Proverbs 30:15. St. Paul beat down his body, 1 Corinthians 9:27. Such a proportion only is to be taken for the recruiting of nature, as may help forward God's service. More are hurt by excess in lawful things than by meddling with unlawful, as more are killed by wine than poison. Many make their belly their god, Philippians 3:19. And to this god, they pour drink offerings. Clemens Alexandrinus writes of a fish whose heart is in its belly—an emblem of epicures whose heart is in their belly; they are devoted to sensualness. Excess in meat or drink clouds the mind, chokes good affections, and provokes lust. The rankest weeds grow out of the fattest soil. Intemperance shortens life as too much oil extinguishes the lamp. Many dig their own graves with their own teeth. Christ cautioned His

Apostles, Luke 21:34, "Take heed to yourselves, lest at
any time your hearts be overcharged with surfeiting
and drunkenness." Seneca could say he was born to
higher things than to be a slave to his body. What a
shame is it that the soul, that princely thing which
sways the scepter of reason and is akin to the angels,
should be enslaved to the brutish part! Deny the sinful
cravings of the flesh. What has God given conscience
for but to be a golden bridle to check the inordinacy of
the appetite?

7. A Christian must deny his ease. Proverbs 1:23:
"Ease slays the simple." The flesh is full of sloth and ef-
feminacy; 'tis loath to take pains for heaven. Proverbs
19:24: "A slothful man hides his hand in his bosom."
He is loath to pluck it out though it is to lay hold on a
crown. Weeds and vermin grow in untilled ground,
and all vices grow in an idle, untilled heart. How can
they expect to reap a harvest of glory who never sowed
any seed? Is Satan so busy in his diocese, 1 Peter 5:8,
and are Christians idle? Are they like the lilies which
toil not, neither do they spin? O deny your ease!
Seneca, a heathen, devoted himself to labor and spent
part of the night in study. Hannibal forced his way over
the Alps and craggy rocks. We must force our way to
paradise. Let us shake off sloth as Paul did the viper.

Never think to be brought to heaven as the passengers in a ship are brought to their ports sleeping.
1 Chronicles 22:16: "Arise and be doing." God puts no
difference between the slothful servant and the wicked,
Matthew 25:26. Those people in Etruria, who like
drones entered into the hive and consumed the honey,
were expelled from others and condemned to exile.

Such as idle away the day of grace and fold their hands
to sleep when they should be working out salvation,
God will condemn to a perpetual exile in hell.

8. A Christian must deny carnal policy. This is the
wisdom of the flesh, 2 Corinthians 1:12. Carnal policy
is craft. The politician does not consult what is best but
what is safest. The politician is made of willow; he can
side with all parties; his religion is cut according to the
fashion of the times; he can bow either to the east or to
the host. Zeal for truth is blotted out of the politician's
creed. It was a speech of Sir Thomas More that he
would not follow truth too near the heels lest it should
dash out his brains. 'Tis judged by some a piece of policy not to declare against error for fear of losing a
party.

The politician is a latitudinarian. He has distinc-
tions beyond Aquinas and can digest those things
which others tremble at. The ostrich's wings help her
to outrun other creatures. Sinful policy makes men
run further than they can who are of purer consciences. In short, the politician is like the chameleon,
who can change into all colors and be as his company
is. He can be either serious or feathery. He can imitate
either Cato or Cataline. I grant that Christian prudence is commendable, but the serpent must not devour the dove. That policy is unjustifiable which
teaches people to avoid duty. Deny carnal policy; dare
to be honest. The best policy is to hold fast to integrity.

9. A Christian must deny his inordinate passions.
James 1:26: "If any man among you seem to be religious, and bridleth not his tongue, this man's religion

is vain." Every member of the body is infected with sin,
as every branch of wormwood is bitter; but the tongue
is full of deadly poison, James 3:8. Augustine compares
the tongue to a furnace, and too often sparks of anger
fly out of it. The Holy Ghost once descended in cloven
tongues of fire, Acts 2:3. But the Apostle James speaks
of a tongue that is set on fire of hell, James 3:6. Some
cannot rule their own spirit, but are carried away with
their passions as a chariot with wild horses. Many, said
Jerome, who will not be drunk with wine will be drunk
with rash anger. Ecclesiastes 7:9: "Anger resteth in the
bosom of fools." Anger may be in a wise man but it
rests in a fool. There is, I know, a holy anger against
sin, but the fury of passion is the scum which boils off
from an unsavory heart. Passion disturbs reason and
make a person unfit for holy duties. Hot passions make
cold prayers.

O Christians, deny yourselves! Pray that God will set
a watch before your lips, Psalm 141:4. Labor to quench
the fire of wrath with a flood of tears. It is recorded of
Mr. John Bruen, in the county of Chester, that though
he was naturally of a hasty, choleric spirit, yet at length
he got the victory over his passions and grew so meek
and calm that his very nature seemed to be quite altered. Grace does to the passions what Christ did to the
sea when it was stormy. In Mark 4 He said, "Peace, be
still." And there was a great calm. Grace turns the
fierceness of the lion into the meekness of the dove.

10. A Christian must deny his sinful fashions.
Romans 12:2: "Be not conformed to this world," to the
guise and mode of it. If the old Christians were to rise
out of their graves, our strange fashions might frighten

them into their graves again. Was there ever such excess in hair? 1 Corinthians 11:14: "If a man have long hair it is a shame." More money is sometimes laid out for a wig to cover one head than would clothe twenty poor persons. One asked Reverend Dod why he did not preach against those ruffians who wore long hair. He replied, "If grace comes into their heart, it will make them cut their hair."

Nor can the female sex be excused for their excess in apparel (see Isaiah 3:19-20). Seneca complained of those in his time who hung two or three patrimonies on their ears. Some wear half their revenues upon their backs. Lysander would not allow his daughters to be too gorgeously attired, saying it would not make them so comely as common. What spotted faces and bare shoulders appear in the congregations! And that professors should conform and comply with others in their antic dresses is the reproach of religion. A tear in the eye would more adorn than a tower on the forehead. O deny yourselves! Pull down these flags of vanity. Have not God's judgments humbled you? 1 Timothy 2:9: "I will therefore that women adorn themselves with modest apparel." Let the hidden man of the heart be beautified and bespangled with grace. Psalm 45:13: "The king's daughter is all glorious within."

11. A Christian must deny His own aims. He must not look with one eye at religion and aim at himself more than God with the other. He must not aim at self-enriching and self-applause.

He must not aim at self-enriching. Some espouse the gospel only for gain. They court this queen not for her beauty but for her jewels. It is not the fire of the

altar they regard but the gold of the altar, 1 Timothy
6:5, supposing that gain is godliness. Camero, a French
divine of Bordeaux, relates a story of one Santangel, a
lawyer, who turned Protestant only out of worldly respects that he might grow rich. Judas preached and
wrought miracles, but his eye was chiefly to the bag.
How do many heap benefice upon benefice, minding
the fleece more than the flock. Dumb dogs are greedy
dogs, Isaiah 56:10-11. These make use of the ministe-
rial function only as a net to catch preferment. This is
to be profane in sacred things. 'Tis sordid and unworthy of a Christian, to make religion bow to secular interest.

A Christian must not aim at self-applause. The
Pharisees were herein guilty who gloried in the creature. They prayed and gave alms that they might be
seen of men, Matthew 6. The oil of vain-glory fed their
lamp. Verse 5: "Verily they have their reward." They
might make their acquittal and write "Received in full
payment." 'Tis a saying of Spanhemius that there is in
every man by nature a spice of Pharisaism, a seeking after the glory and applause of the world. Luther con-
fessed that, though he was never tempted with covetousness, yet he was sometimes with vain-glory.
Christ's own disciples were disputing who should be
the greatest, Mark 9:34. O this devil of vain-glory! The
moth breeds in the finest cloth, and self-seeking is apt
to breed in the best duties. Sinister aims corrupt religion. A good aim will not make a bad action good, but
a bad aim will make a good action bad.

To blame are they who, when they have done any
glorious service in the church, take the praise to themselves, like those heathens who sacrificed the wax to

their gods but kept the honey to themselves. Matthew Paris speaks of one who, having in several lectures proved strenuously that Christ was God, and being highly applauded for it, cried out saying, "O Jesus, Thou art beholden to me for Thy divinity this day." Whereupon this doctor was stricken suddenly with such stupidness and forgetfulness that he could never afterwards say the Lord's Prayer unless a little child said it to him.

Let this cause trembling and humility in Christians. Several ships which have escaped the rocks have been cast away upon the sands. Many who have escaped the rocks of gross scandals have been cast away upon the sands of self-seeking. Tacitus said he would not have Erasmus's fame and applause for all the world. No, but to have esteem in God's church is a blessing. Hebrews 11:2: "By faith the elders obtained a good report." Much of the honor of religion depends upon the credit of those who profess it. But the sin is when self-applause is the only thing hunted after. Popular acclamation is a golden arrow which glitters in the eye but wounds the heart. How many have been blown to hell with the breath of popular applause!

O let us deny, yea, abhor this vain-glorious humour. We have a famous example in John the Baptist, who sought to lift up Christ and beat down himself. John 1:15: "He that cometh after Me is preferred before me." It is as if he had said, "I am but the herald, the voice of one crying. Christ, who comes after me, is the Prince. I am but the morning star; He is the sun. I baptize only with water, He with the Holy Ghost." Thus he sets the crown of honor upon Christ's head. When Joab had taken Rabbah, he did not arrogate the praise to himself, but sent for King David that he might carry away the glory of the victory, 2 Samuel 12:27. So when any eminent service in church or state has been done, the glory of all should be given to Christ and free grace. It is better that God should approve than that the world should applaud. If we are faithful we shall have honor enough in heaven. Let this be our chief aim in duty that we may grow more in love with God and be made more like Him, have more communion with Him, and bring more revenues of honor to Him. 1 Peter 4:11: "That in all things, God may be glorified." We should not only advance but design God's glory. It was a worthy speech of Philip de Mornay upon his deathbed, that he had, through the course of his life, made God's glory his end and aim. As all the rivers run into the sea, so all our actions must run into God, the infinite Ocean.

12. A Christian must deny all ungodliness. Titus 2:11-12: "The grace of God hath appeared to all men, teaching us that denying ungodliness and worldly lusts, we should live soberly." The Turks say in their Koran that God did not give men lustful desires to be frustrated. But let their Koran go with the Papist's "Legend." The Scripture seals no patents for sin. It bids us deny ungodly lusts. It is not likely he will sacrifice his Isaac, his worldly profits, who will not sacrifice the ram, his vile lusts. A Christian must deny his malice, revenge, covetousness, uncleanness, superstition, and heterodoxy. A man may as well go to hell for a drunken opinion as a drunken life. And let me especially instance two sins a Christian must deny:
The sin of rash censuring. James 4:11: "Speak not evil

one of another." Some make it a part of their religion to criticize others and clip their credit to make it weigh lighter. You shall hear them say, "Such a one is proud, factious, and hypocritical." James 4:12: "Who art thou that judgest another?" Augustine could not endure that any should detract from the good name of others.

The root of censoriousness is pride. A person thinks that by taking another's reputation he shall add something to our own. But let him who shall raise himself upon the ruin of another's fame look to it. Do you think it is no sin to murder a man in his name? You who are such a critic, it is to be feared you can spy all faults but your own. O Christian, look inward. If you viewed your own spots more in the looking glass of the Word, you would not be as ready to throw the stone of censure at others. Deny this sin of rash censuring or smiting with the tongue, Jeremiah 18:18. You who speak reproachfully of your brother without a cause, the time may come that he may be accepted and you rejected. He may be found gold and you reprobate silver.

A Christian must deny his complexion sin. Psalm 12:23: "I have kept myself from mine iniquity." As there is one master bee in the hive, so there is naturally one master sin in the heart. This must be denied. The devil can hold a man fast by one sin. A jailer can hold the prisoner fast by one fetter. One sin is enough to stop the current of mercy. One sin may damn as well as more, just as one millstone is enough to sink a man into the sea. If there be any lust which we cannot deny, it will be a bitter root either of scandal or apostasy.

13. A Christian must deny his relations. Luke 14:26: "If any man come to me and hate not father and mother and wife and children, he cannot be My disciple." The meaning is, when carnal relations come in competition with, or stand in opposition to, Christ, we must hate them. When our friends would prove snares and hinder us from our duty, we must either leap over them or tread upon them. Here is faith in God. If my wife, said Jerome, should hang about my neck, if my mother should show me her breasts that gave me suck, and persuade me to deny Christ, I would break from them and fly to the cross. When Peter would be a tempter, Christ said, "Get thee behind Me, Satan."

14. A Christian must deny his estate for Christ. A carnal heart will commend and profess Christ, but will part with nothing for Him. The young man in the gospel was Christ's hearer but not His follower. He had heavenly desires but an earthly appetite, as one has said. When Christ said to him, "Sell all and give to the poor," he went away sorrowful, Matthew 19:22. When Mercury is in conjunction with a bad planet, it has a bad influence. So, when riches are joined with a bad heart, they do much hurt.

The world lay nearer the young man's heart than Christ. Have some of the heathens denied the world? Epaminondas, a Grecian captain who obtained many glorious victories, was a great condemner of the world. He refused vast sums of money sent him from the King of Persia, so that when he died he left scarcely enough to defray the charges of his funeral. Did a heathen go thus far in denying the world, and shall not Christians do much more? Let the wedge of gold be denied for the pearl of price. Matthew 19:27: "We have forsaken all and followed Thee." A true saint esteems the gleanings of Christ better than the world's vintage. Philippians 3:8: "For whom I have suffered the loss of all things." Galeacius, marquess of Vico, parted with a fair estate to enjoy the pure ordinances of Christ at Geneva. When a Jesuit persuaded him to return to his popish religion in Italy, promising him a huge sum of money, he said, "Let their money perish with them, who esteem all the gold in the world worth one hour's communion with Jesus Christ and His Holy Spirit."

15. A Christian must deny his life for Christ. This is in the text, "Let him take up his cross." Suffering for Christ must be free and spontaneous. He who suffers against his will bears the cross; he who suffers willingly takes up the cross. A fair virgin fell in love with Crates for his learning. He showed her his staff and his scrip. "This," he said, "is your dowry." Christ shows us His cross. If we will not have Him upon these terms, the match is not likely to go on. Sufferings will abide us, Acts 20:23 and 2 Timothy 3:12. The devil has not grown kinder than he was.

Some think of reigning with Christ, but not of suffering. Joseph dreamed of his advancement but not of his imprisonment.

The flesh cries out, "The cross is uneasy! There are nails in the yoke that tear."

But life must be denied, yea, hated for Christ. Luke 14:26: "If any man come to Me and hate not father and mother and his own life, he cannot be My disciple." Love for Christ must outweigh life. Revelation 12:11:

"They loved not their lives to the death." Paul carried the image of Christ in his heart as a saint, the message of Christ in his mouth as a minister, and the marks of Christ in his body as a martyr, Galatians 6:17. The primitive worthies snatched up torments as so many crowns and were content to shed their blood for Christ, knowing they would exchange their sanguine for white robes. The prophet Isaiah was killed with a saw, Jeremiah with stones, Amos with an iron bar. Luke was hanged on an olive tree.

I read that Irenaeus was carried to a place where a cross was set on one side and an idol on the other. He was given a choice either to bow to the idol or suffer on the cross. He chose the latter.

Basil speaks of a virgin condemned to the fire. She was offered her life and estate if she would bow down to an image. She answered, "Let life and money go; welcome Christ."

Though every Christian is not actually a martyr, yet he has a preparation of mind and is ready to suffer if God calls. Luther said he would rather be a martyr than a monarch. Let us then take up the cross.

Can wicked men be content to suffer for their lusts, and shall we not suffer for Christ? We are to look upon our sufferings as a badge of honor. If we receive honor when we are reproached for Christ, much more shall we receive it when we die for Him. 1 Peter 4:14: "A spirit of God and of glory resteth upon us." Our sufferings for Christ propagate religion. Paul's being bound made the gospel to be more enlarged, Philippians 1:12. Justin Martyr was converted to the faith by beholding the heroic patience and courage of the Christians in their sufferings.

The cross leads to the crown. 2 Timothy 2:12: "If we suffer, we shall also reign with Him." Who would not be willing to venture on the seas, though rough and tempestuous, if he were sure to be crowned as soon as he came ashore? Persecutors may take away from us our goods but not our God; our liberty but not our freedom of conscience; our head but not our crown, Revelation 2:10.

He who cannot deny his life for Christ will deny Christ. And he who is ashamed of Christ, Christ will be ashamed of him. Mark 8:38: "Whosoever shall be ashamed of Me and My words in this adulterous and sinful generation, of him shall the Son of Man be ashamed when He cometh in the glory of His Father with His holy angels."

Chapter 3

Containing the Ground of the Proposition

The grand reason why we must deny ourselves is because we can be saved no other way. A town or castle may have several ways leading to it, but there is but one way leading to the celestial paradise, and that is self-denial. Without self-denial, we can never come up to Christ's terms. If the world cannot be denied, Christ cannot be loved. If self-righteousness cannot be denied, Christ cannot be trusted. If the will is not denied, Christ cannot be obeyed. Therefore, self-denial is of as absolute necessity as heaven.

Chapter 4

An Inference Drawn from the Proposition

From all that has been said, see how hard a thing it is to be a Christian. Were it only to put on the mantle of profession, it would be easy. Even Satan can transform himself into an angel of light, 2 Corinthians 11:14. But a man must deny himself. This self-emptying or self-annihilation is the strait gate through which a Christian must enter into the kingdom of God. He is not to deny only those things which are outside him, his worldly profits, but those which are within him, his sins, nay, his righteousness. Self is an idol, and it is hard to sacrifice this idol; but this must be done. Either carnal self must be denied or natural self denied.

Chapter 5

A Check to Epicures and Sensualists

This justly indicts those who live in a contradiction to the text, who instead of denying themselves let loose the reins and give themselves up to all manner of pleasure and licentiousness. Ecclesiastes 7:4: "The heart of fools is in the house of mirth." Such the prophet deciphers, who do not mortify but gratify the flesh. Amos 6:4-5: "That lie upon beds of ivory, and stretch themselves upon their couches, that chant to the sound of the vial, that drink wine in bowls." Pleasure, like Circe, enchants men's minds and transforms them into beasts.

There is a place in Africa called Tombutium where the inhabitants spend all their time in piping and dancing. And have we not many who consume their hours in plays and brothels? As if God had made them like the leviathan, in Psalm 104:26, to play in the water. How will their countenances be changed when God shall say, "Give an account of your stewardship!" These frolicking sensualists live as if there were no world to come. They pamper their bodies but starve their souls. As if one should feed his slave but starve his wife.

Do epicures deny themselves? Indeed, in one sense they do. Enjoying their lusts, they deny themselves a part in heaven. In the country of Sardinia there is an herb-like balm that if a man eats of it he shall die laughing. Such an herb is pleasure. If one feeds immoderately on it, he will go laughing to hell. Esau lost the blessing while he was hunting. O! How many, while they are hunting after worldly pleasures, lose blessedness? There is a sin cup brewing which will spoil the sinner's mirth. Psalm 75:8: "In the hand of the Lord there is a cup, the wine is red, it is full of mixture." This wine is the wrath of God, and it is mixed; the worm and the fire help to mix the cup. The Lord will proportion a sinner's torment to his pleasure. Revelation 18:7: "How much she hath lived deliciously, so much torment and sorrow give her."

Chapter 6

The Lack of Self-Denial Lamented

In the next place, we may sadly lay to heart the lack of self-denial. O self-denial, where have you gone? We live in a knowing age, yet few know how to deny themselves. Selfishness is the reigning sin of the world. This makes the times have a bad aspect. 2 Timothy 3:1-2: "Perilous times shall come, for men shall be lovers of themselves."

Self may have divers actions brought against it. It is an enemy to the public. James 4:1: "Whence come wars?" Whence is robbery and bribery? Whence is oppression and circumvention but from those selfish lusts which men cannot conquer? When Lentulus had declared Tiberius Caesar to be his heir in his will, so basely selfish was Caesar that he sent and killed Lentulus that he might have immediate possession of his goods.

Self-denial lodges but in a few breasts. It is a sacred, exotic herb which has grown very scarce. Luke 18:8: "When the Son of Man cometh, shall He find faith on the earth?" May it not be said, "Shall He find self-denial on the earth?" Self-denial has gone on a long pilgrimage, and who can tell when it will return?

Chapter 7

Containing a Persuasive to Self-Denial

My next work is to persuade Christians to the practice of this momentous duty of self-denial. Man lost himself at first by self-exaltation, and he must recover himself by self-denial.

1. *Self-denial is just and equal.* How much has Christ denied Himself for us? He eclipsed His glory, Philippians 2:7: "He denied Himself." What wonderful self-denial was it for Christ to leave His Father's bosom and be incarnate? For Christ to be made flesh was more than for all the angels to be made worms. Christ denied His name and reputation, Hebrews 12:2: "He endured the shame." He denied worldly grandeurs and riches. 1 Corinthians 8:9: "For our sakes He became poor." The manger was His cradle, the cobwebs His curtains. He denied His life, Philippians 2:8: "He became obedient to death." 'Tis but equity we should deny ourselves for Christ.

2. *Self-denial is the sign of a sincere Christian.* Hypocrites may have great knowledge and make fair pretenses, but it is only the sincere saint who can deny himself and lay his life at Christ's feet. This was a touchstone of Moses' sincerity. He denied the pleasures of the court and chose affliction rather than iniquity, Hebrews 11:25.

I have read of a holy man who was once tempted by

Satan. Satan said to him, "Why do you take all these
pains? What do you more than I? Are you no drunk-
ard, no adulterer? No more am I. Do you watch? I
never sleep. Do you fast? I never eat. What do you
more than I?"

"Why," said the good man, "I tell you, Satan, I give
myself to prayer, nay, more, I deny myself."

"Nay," said the devil, "you go beyond me, for I exalt
myself." And so he vanished.

3. *Self-denial is a rational thing.* For if self is an enemy
then it is wisdom to discard it. There is a rationality in
all God's commands. Why would He have us deny
fleshly lusts but because they wage war against our
souls? 1 Peter 2:11. Why would He have us deny pride
but because of its noxious quality? Proverbs 16:18:
"Pride goeth before destruction." Where pride leads
the van, destruction brings up the rear. God would
have us deny nothing for him but that which will damn
us if we keep it.

4. *There is nothing lost by self-denial.* We shall be
abundantly compensated. Matthew 19:29: "Everyone
that hath forsaken houses and lands for My sake shall
receive an hundredfold, and shall inherit life
everlasting." If we deny our name and reputation for
Christ, God will give us inward peace. There is "an
hundredfold" in this life, and He will honor us before
the angels. How many hundredfolds that amounts to I
am not able to tell. If we deny our estate to keep our
conscience, God will give us a kingdom, Luke 12:32.
What does he lose who parts with a flower and gets a
jewel? We may lose all we have for Christ, yet lose
nothing by Him.

Chapter 8

Containing Helps to Self-Denial

For the attaining of self-denial, let these rules be observed:

1. *Be convinced of the incomparable excellency of Christ.* He has an equality and consubstantiality with God the Father, Colossians 2:9. He is the quintessence of goodness. He is compared to a head of gold for riches, Song of Solomon 5:10; to the Rose of Sharon for perfume, Song of Solomon 2:1; to a bright morning star for beauty, Revelation 22:16. Jesus Christ is all that God can require for satisfaction or that we can desire for salvation. He is fully commensurate to our wants. He has eye salve to anoint us, white raiment to cover us, and His blood to heal us.

We shall never deny ourselves for Christ until we see a glory and a beauty in Him. Christ is all marrow and sweetness. He is better than life, estate, or heaven.

2. *Endeavor after a vital principle of grace.* Grace will do that which flesh and blood cannot. A man may do that by art which he cannot do by strength. A burden of great weight may be lifted up by screws and pulleys which cannot be lifted up by strength of arm. Grace will teach one the art of self-denial which cannot be done by strength of nature. In particular, labor for three graces.

Humility. A proud man admires himself; therefore

he cannot deny himself. A humble man lays his mouth
in the dust. He has lower thoughts of himself than
others can have of him. He goes out of himself. He re-
nounces himself. He opens to God as the flower does
to the sun. He will do what God will have him do. He
will be what God will have him be. He is like melting
wax. God may set what stamp and impression He will
upon him. The humble man is the self-denier.

Love. Who will not deny himself for a friend whom
he loves? He will part with anything he has. He will
gratify him whom he loves, though it is to his own loss.
He whose heart is fired with love for Christ will stop at
nothing for His sake. Gregory Nazianzen said of his
Athenian learning that he was glad he had anything of
worth to esteem as nothing for Christ. Love for God
will devour self-love.

Faith. Abraham was a great self-denier. He left his
kindred and country and was willing to travel to any
place where God would have him. Whence was this? It
was from his faith. Hebrews 11:8: "By faith Abraham
obeyed and went out, not knowing whither he went."
He who believes that Christ and heaven are his, what
will he not relinquish for Christ's sake? The stronger a
Christian's faith is, the more eminent will his self-denial be.

3. *Pray much for self-denial.* Prayer sets God to work,
Psalm 10:17. Some pray for assurance but lack self-denial, as if God would set seal to a blank. Let this be
your grand request, a self-denying frame of heart. Self-
denial does not grow in nature, it is a fruit of the Spirit.
Beg God that he will plant this heavenly flower in your
soul. Say, "Lord, whatever Thou deniest me, deny me
not self-denial. Let me rather lack great parts, nay, let

me rather lack the comforts of the Spirit than self-denial."

There may be going to heaven without comfort, but there is no going there without self-denial.

The Comforting Rod

"Thy rod and Thy staff, they comfort me."
Psalm 23:4

This Psalm St. Bernard calls a noble and illustrious Psalm. The Jews used to repeat this Psalm when they sat down to their meat. In it, David sets forth two things: his experience and his confidence. His confidence, in the first and last verses. In the first verse, "The Lord is my Shepherd; (therefore) I shall not want." In the last verse, "Surely goodness and mercy shall follow me all the days of my life." Here is David's confidence. His faith was risen up into a great degree of confidence. But that which I shall speak to is David's experience in the words I have read: "Thy rod and Thy staff, they comfort me."

What is meant here by staff? A staff is for support, whether it be the staff one walks with to support the body or whether it be the staff of bread that supports the life of man. Staff is for support, and so it is used here in the text, "Thy staff comforts me." By staff is meant, metaphorically, the staff of God's support: "Thy staff comforts me." God's providence is a wing to cover the saints. It is a breast to feed them and a staff to uphold them. In the most calamitous times, the Church of God has the staff of God's support, and this is the reason that the Church is preserved in spite of all malice and opposition. This bush burns, yet it is not consumed. Though the lion roars, yet the lambs of Christ's fold are in safety. Though the rulers take counsel against the saints of the Most High, yet they are kept alive. Here is the reason Thy staff comforts me. The saints always have the staff of divine protection. God secretly preserves them and sets an invisible guard about them. We see the staff that smites the godly, but we do not see the staff that upholds them. We see their danger but do not see their defense. God is their staff of support. God's continual care of His Church is as a wall of brass against which the gates of hell shall never prevail. The Church of God has God for her Guardian. The enemies must first overcome God before they can overcome His Church, said Luther.

For the use of this briefly: This is no small comfort to God's Church. She has a staff of support. God is her protection. The saints of God have malignant enemies to conflict with. The powers of the earth are against the godly. We read that the beast in Revelation had on his head seven horns and ten crowns, Revelation 13:1: "And this was given him to make war with the saints." You see, the people of God were then in an ill case. They had the horns and the crowns against them. But the saints have the Lion of the tribe of Judah on their side. And Christ has a staff to protect them and teeth to devour all His enemies.

So much briefly for that expression, for I have only glanced at it. "Thy staff doth comfort me." Thy staff of support and glorious providence is always with me. It comforts me.

But that which I shall chiefly speak to is the first of these in the text, "Thy rod doth comfort me."

In the opening of this the question is:

QUESTION. What is meant by rod?

ANSWER. This word rod, when it is ascribed to God, is taken three ways in Scripture.

First, for God's destroying rod.

Second, for God's pastoral rod, as that of a shepherd.

Third, for his disciplining rod, or rod of affliction.

1. The rod, when it is ascribed unto God, which He uses towards His enemies. Psalm 12:9: "Thou shalt break them with a rod of iron." This rod of God upon His enemies comforts the godly, Psalm 58:10. The righteous shall rejoice when they see the vengeance. God's destroying rod upon sinners is a matter of rejoicing and comfort unto the godly. We read of Deborah's triumphant song and the Jew's festival after the destruction of Haman, Esther 9:22. The rod of God upon the wicked comforts the godly.

QUESTION. But some may say, "How far may the godly be comforted in the destruction of wicked men? How far may they rejoice?"

ANSWER. The godly may be comforted in the destruction of wicked men so far as now there is a stop put to their sins, and they cannot live any longer to dishonor God.

Second, God's destroying rod upon the wicked is a matter of comfort to the godly as hereby God's justice is declared to all the world. Why did God smite Pharaoh? For his pride and tyranny. The saints rejoice and triumph to see God's justice executed upon His enemies, Exodus 15:1. They are comforted to see God's justice in punishing the wicked of the world.

Third, it is comfort to the people of God to see a wicked man destroyed. God's ruining of sinners is a warning to others to make them fear sin. This is clear from Deuteronomy 17:12-13. The man who does presumptuously shall die, and all the people shall hear and fear and do no more presumptuously. God's judgments upon wicked persecutors may make others afraid and tremble to go on in their sin. Thus far God's destroying rod is a comfort to the godly. They rejoice to think that this may be a warning to sinners, and may be a means to reclaim many from their impieties.

Fourth, and last, God's destroying rod upon the wicked is a comfort to the godly upon this account, as peace and deliverance arises to the Church of God. When Pharaoh was destroyed, Israel had a writ of ease now granted them. Nay, further, the destruction of the wicked, such as are desperate sinners, not only causes liberty to arise in the Church of God, but it causes the growth of religion. A clear instance: Herod being eaten up with worms, the text says immediately that "the Word of God grew and multiplied," Acts 12:23. Thus far God's destroying rod upon the wicked, flagitious sinners is a comfort to the godly. "Thy rod doth comfort me." Thy rod of iron that breaks the profane sinners of the world comforts me.

2. As there is God's destroying rod which comforts the godly, so there is God's pastoral rod which He uses towards His sheep, conducting them to green pastures and still waters. There is God's shepherd rod by which He leads His elect sheep to the green pastures and still waters. These green pastures and still waters may be meant of the ordinances and that sweet comfort the

people of God find in the use of them. Why, this rod of
God, this shepherd's rod, this pastoral rod, comforts
the godly.

3. Third, and last, there is God's disciplining rod,
or His rod of affliction. This also is a comfort to the
people of God. 2 Samuel 7:14: "I will chasten him with
a rod of Mine." And in Micah 6:9, "Hear ye the rod,
and who hath appointed it." And in this sense I understand this text of Scripture, "Thy rod doth comfort
me." So, then, the observation is this:
**DOCTRINE: God's rod, His afflicting rod upon
His people, yields matter of comfort to us.**
"Thy rod doth comfort me." This, I confess, to flesh
and blood seems a paradox; it seems strange. What,
that the rod of correction should give comfort! If
David had said, "Thy promises, Lord, they comfort
me," it would have been no wonder. But that he should
say, "Thy rod doth comfort me," how can this be? Is it
usual for the Church to call pain comfort? How, then,
does David say, "Thy rod doth comfort me"? Who can
of such thistles gather figs? Or of such thorns gather
grapes? How can there be comfort from the rod?
I shall show you that there is much consolation
gathered out of correction. "Thy rod doth comfort
me." The rod of God is not like Moses' rod when
turned into a serpent, but it is like Jonathan's rod
which had honey at the end of it. The rod of God is
like Aaron's rod which brought forth buds, blossoms,
and almonds, Numbers 17:8.
Then the question is this: How does this afflicting
rod give comfort?
In six particulars.

How God's Afflicting Rod Comforts Us

1. *God's afflicting rod comforts us as it gives us instruction.* Where it teaches it comforts. Micah 7:14: "Teach Thy people with Thy rod." How does the rod teach? Why, it teaches with instruction, so it teaches with comfort. Luther said there were many Psalms in the Bible he never rightly understood until he was in affliction. The rod teaches to know God aright, and is that not matter of comfort? In 2 Chronicles 33:11, when Manasseh was afflicted, then he knew the Lord was God. And the rod teaches a man to know himself. He sees that corruption working in his heart that he could never discern before. The eyes that sin shuts affliction opens. The rod gives wisdom; it is a teaching rod, and thus God comforts. What if it makes us weaker, so long as it makes us wiser?

2. *God's afflicting rod has comfort in it as it is a token of special favor He bears towards us, Revelation 13:19.* We think God cannot favor us unless He has us in His lap. Yet He loves and favors us when He gives us the bitter diet-drink of affliction. God's rod and God's love both stand together. Thus the rod comforts; it brings us a token of God's love. It is no love in God to let men go on in sin and never smite; this is no love. Is it any love to your child to let him take his course and run into the water and drown if he will? To be without the rod of God's discipline is a sign of a bastard child, a mark of reprobation, Hebrews 12:8. If God will let any fall upon the rock of ruin, then He will allow them to go on in sin and not correct them. Hosea 4:14: "I will not punish your daughters when they commit whoredom." Take notice, God spares the rod in anger. God's hand

is heaviest when it is lightest. God punishes most when
He does not punish. But now God smites that He may
save His people, and is that not love? And the love of
God allays and takes off the smarting power of the rod
and gives the soul comfort. Let me feel God's hand so I
may have his heart.

3. *God's rod comforts as it makes way for comfort.*
Medicine, though bitter, yet has comfort in it as it
makes way for health. The rod is to make way for comfort. The rod of God is to beat out the dust and make
us purer. If a clothmaker dips his cloth in water it is to
whiten the cloth. The water of afflictions is to make
God's people white. Daniel 12:10: "Many shall be tried
and made white."

Nay, farther, God's rod upon His children not only
makes way for comfort but, what is more, this rod distills comfort into the soul. Even as the fire causes sweet
water to drop from the still, so out of affliction God
stills the sweet water of consolation. A clear instance is
in 2 Corinthians 1:4: "Who comforteth us in all our
tribulations." Here is the rod of God comforting.
When the saints' trials have been sharpest, their comforts have been sweetest. Behold here honey at the end
of the rod. John 16:22: "Your sorrows shall be turned
into joy." Here is the saints' water turned into wine.
That holy martyr who was in prison dates his letter
thus: "From the pleasant garden of the lion prison."
God candies His wormwood with sugar. The saints
never tasted so much of God's compassion as in their
deepest affliction. And in this sense David might truly
say, "Thy rod doth comfort me." So said the Apostle,
"God comforteth us in all our tribulations."

4. *God's afflicting rod has comfort in it as it brings the*

good news to the soul that this is the worst that shall
ever befall him. The Lord comes down with a murder-
ing axe to hew down wicked men, but He has only a
rattling rod to His children. This is all the hell they
ever shall feel. Is this not comfort? 1 Corinthians 11:32:
"But when we are judged, we are chastened of the
Lord that we should not be condemned with this
world." Is this not comfort to know that this is the worst
we shall have? God lays upon us a light affliction and
saves us from wrath to come. Here is the rod full of
comfort. What is a drop of sorrow that the godly taste
to the bottomless sea of wrath the damned endure forever?

5. *Yet farther, the rod is full of comfort as it makes us
happy*. And for this consult Job 5:17, "Behold, happy is
that man whom God correcteth."

Among the philosophers, some place their happiness in riches, some in wisdom, some in pleasure and
the like, but who ever placed happiness in affliction?

The worldlings cry, "If this is happiness, Lord, deliver me from it!" But Job said, "Happy is that man
whom God correcteth." How is he happy? He is happy
who is made better by affliction. Though the cross
makes the outward condition worse, yet it makes the
heart better.

Again, he is happy who has God to visit him. Don't
we account him a happy person who has a king to visit
him? How much more to have a God to visit him?
Persecution is a rod, yea, but for all that it is a blessed
rod, it is a healing rod. Though a rod smarts, yet it
saves the soul. Well, then, may a Christian say, "Lord,
Thy rod comforts me. This makes me happy." Happy is
that man whom God corrects.

6. *Last, God's rod has comfort in it as a means to bring us to glory.* God's rod whips us to heaven. 2 Corinthians 4:17: "These light afflictions, which are but for a moment, work for us a far more exceeding and eternal weight of glory." Affliction is like throwing a bag of money at another person; it may bruise him, but it enriches him. So affliction may bruise us but it enriches us, and this works for us a far more exceeding and eternal weight of glory.

In short, the black rod prepares for the white rod. O Christian! You who are now humbled by some sharp affliction shall shortly wear a garland made of the flowers of paradise. You shall have your soul set thicker with the jewels of heaven than the firmament is with the stars.

Thus you see this truth is verified, "Thy rod doth comfort me."

Application

USE 1. OF INFERENCE. I will name but four:

1. *See then from hence the difference between the wicked and the godly.* God makes the worst things tend to the consolation of the godly and the best things tend to the condemnation of the wicked. Let the people of God meet with affliction, it is for the better. God's rod comforts. Let the wicked have prosperity, it is for the worse. Cordials themselves kill them. To the godly, evil things have good in them. To the wicked, good things have hurt in them. This is clear Scripture, "Their table is a snare." I say, the wicked's table is a snare, Psalm 69:22. Wicked men have mercy out of God's hand as

Israel had quails. They were sauced with the wrath of God. Ecclesiastes 5:13, a clear Scripture: "I have seen an evil under the sun, riches kept for owners to their hurt." Riches are like Haman's banquet, which was a prologue to his execution. To wicked men, even spiritual mercies are turned into judgments. The Word preached is a savor of death to the wicked, 2 Corinthians 2:16. Nay, farther, Jesus Christ Himself is a rock of offense to the wicked, 1 Peter 2:7. Christ is equally for the falling as the rising of many in Israel, Luke 2:34. In short, sinners stumble at a Savior and pluck death from the tree of life. As for the godly, God's rod comforts them. As for the wicked, God's mercy ruins them.

2. *See then from hence that religion is not to be looked on as a melancholy thing.* Some persons discourage religion and draw it with a sour countenance and in a frightful dress. But we see the worst of religion has much comfort in it. The very rod of God comforts the godly. See the Scripture in James 1:2, "Account it, my brethren, all joy when you fall into divers temptations." That is, afflictions are called temptations because they are for trial. "Account it all joy," that is, joy and all joy. Take the part of religion that is sourest to the soul, repentance, and that which is sour to the body, affliction, and there is comfort in both.

There is comfort in that which is sour to the soul, repentance. For whom is the oil of joy prepared but for God's mourners? Isaiah 61:3. A gracious soul is never more enlarged and comforted than when he can melt kindly for sin. Christ Jesus made the best wine from water. The best wine of joy is made of the water of true repentance. The Hebrew word for repentance signifies to take comfort. None have such ground of comfort as a true penitent. When God makes him weep for sin, he goes away weeping for joy. Thus you see the sourest part of religion has comfort in it. Take that which is sour to the body, affliction, and it has comfort in it. A parallel Scripture for this is worth observing. 2 Corinthians 6:20: "As sorrowful, yet always rejoicing." There is comfort in the rod. A Christian is like a bird that can sing in the winter season. He can pick comfort out of the rod and, with Samson, fetch honey out of the lion. 1 Thessalonians 1:6: "Having received the Word with much affliction, with joy." Here is God's rod comforting that Christian who knows affliction tends to better him, making his grace purer and his crown brighter. He can rejoice in affliction and say as David, "O Lord, Thy rod comforts me." Thus, you see, religion is no uncheerful thing.

3. *If God's rod comforts, then it shows us what good reason we have to choose affliction rather than sin.* There is something in affliction to comfort us, but there is nothing in sin to comfort us. Sin is evil and nothing but evil. It is the spirit of witchcraft. It defiles the mind and disturbs the peace. It puts a worm into conscience, a sting into death, and a fire into hell. This is, in Scripture, called "the abominable thing," Jeremiah 44:4: "Do not this abominable thing which I hate." Sin binds the soul over unto God's wrath forever. Oh, then, what wisdom is it to choose affliction rather than sin! A Christian can say, "There is comfort in the rod," but he cannot say, "There is comfort in sin." Sin puts the soul into an agony and makes it the very suburbs of hell. Moses chose affliction rather than sin for a season, Hebrews 11:25.

4. *Last, if God's rod comforts, then what does God's love*

do? If there is any comfort, as you have heard, while God is afflicting us, what comfort is there while He is embracing us? If there is any comfort in the valley of tears, what is there then in paradise? There is the bed of spices and the river of pleasures. If God can make a prison sweet, what then is heaven? If afflicting mercy is so great, what is crowning mercy? If God made one of the martyr's flames a bed of roses, why then, how sweet is it to lie in Christ's bosom, the bed of perfume?

USE 2. OF EXHORTATION.

If God's rod has so much comfort in it to the godly, then be not too much dejected and cast down in affliction. If you meet with losses, if you meet with pirates at sea and hornets on land, you see God can turn all these to good. "Thy rod comforts me." Therefore, be not too much cast down. Though we are not to pray for affliction, for it is in itself penal, neither must we despond under affliction.

"Oh," said one, "if God loved me, He would not have dealt this severely with me. He has bereaved me of such and such a dear comfort, which is like plucking a limb from the body."

But Christian, consider that which you call a dear comfort that God has taken away. Perhaps it was an idol. It may be you loved it more than you did God; and if you had not lost this comfort, you might have lost your soul and heaven too. Why then, has God done you any wrong in taking away this comfort? There is mercy in all this. May you not say at last, "Thy rod comforts me"?

USE 3. OF TRIAL.

Let us examine whether we have had any honey out of the lion, any comfort out of affliction. Has the rod of God upon us blossomed and brought forth almonds? It's certain we have met with affliction in one kind or another, but what benefit have we got by affliction? What advantage for our souls? Can we say indeed as David, "Lord, Thy rod comforts me"? Can we say that we have met with such and such a sore trial, and it has brought us nearer to God and weaned us from the world? that it has conquered our pride and tamed our covetousness? When God's rod upon us fetches water of tears and makes us weep bitterly for our sin, then it is a good rod.

In short, if God's rod has made us better, it has made us reform and break off iniquity. This is when we can say with Ephraim, Hosea 14:8, "What have I to do with idols?"

To conclude all, let it be our daily prayer to God that we may find some comfort in affliction, some honey mingled with our gall. David speaks of comfort in affliction, Psalm 119:50: "This is my comfort in affliction." Affliction is not joyous but grievous. Oh, but when the Lord blesses and sanctifies it to us, then it brings comfort with it.

Let us pray that we may hear the voice of the rod and kiss the rod and bless the hand that holds it. Let us pray unto God that we may see His hand in every affliction and wherefore God contends with us that we may turn to him who smites and say, as David does here in the text, "Oh, Lord, Thy rod and Thy staff, they comfort me."

The Peace of Christ

"These things have I spoken unto you, that in Me ye might have peace: In the world ye shall have tribulation, but be of good cheer; I have overcome the world." John 16:33

These words were spoken by our blessed Savior not long before His suffering. The chapters foregoing are full of spiritual sweetness. This blessed Sun of righteousness, it seems, shone more glorious and brightly a little before His setting. Our Savior Christ was now about to leave the world and go to His Father. And therefore, having endeavored to comfort the hearts of His apostles and disciples, He knew they would be sorrowful. Therefore He endeavors the more to comfort them; and this is the great cordial He gave them before His death: "These things I have spoken unto you, that in Me ye might have peace."

Christ foretold that sufferings would befall His apostles and disciples. "In the world," said He, "ye shall have tribulation." The Greek word for tribulation is a metaphor that alludes to grapes that are squeezed in the wine-press until the blood of the grapes comes out. So, said Christ, "In the world ye shall have tribulation." You shall be put into the wine-press and, perhaps, the blood of the grape may be pressed out. Tribulation is the saints' diet-drink; it is bitter but it is wholesome. All that God does in afflicting His children is but to make

51

them better, and to try them and make them white, Daniel 10:12. Is it not far better to swim through the main river, the Red Sea of affliction, to heaven than to swim through the perfumed joys and pleasures to hell and damnation? "In the world," said Christ, "you must look for, and you shall have tribulation." But Christ, having told of this bitter pill, gives them some sugar of comfort to sweeten it and make it go down better. In the words of this text, "These things I have told you, that in Me ye might have peace."

First, here is the dark side of the cloud: tribulation.

Second, here is the bright side of the cloud: that "in Me ye might have peace."

DOCTRINE: The Lord Jesus Christ, who is our Peacemaker, gives His sweet peace to all His people.

The peace meant here in the text is spiritual and sacred. It is the immediate fruit and product of our justification. Romans 5:1: "Being justified by faith, we have peace with God." This spiritual peace the Lord Jesus procures by His blood, conveys by His Spirit, and maintains by His intercession.

First, this peace is purchased and procured by His blood. It swims to us in the blood of Christ. The justice of God being wronged by us, Jesus Christ laid down His life as a price. He paid that for our peace. It is His blood that cements us and reconciles us to God the Father. Colossians 1:20: "Having made peace through the blood of Jesus."

Second, Christ conveys this blessed peace by His Spirit. He procures it by His merit and He conveys it by His Spirit, John 16:7. The Lord Jesus left this peace to us as a legacy. And the Spirit is Christ's executor to see that His will is made good and that we should have this peace. And now that God is at peace with us through Christ, conscience is at peace too. If the heavens are quiet and serene, and there is no tempest there or wind blowing, then the sea is calm. So, if the great God is at peace with us, and there is no tempest in His face, then conscience is quiet and all is calm.

Third, as Christ procures this blessed peace by His blood and conveys it by His Spirit, so He maintains this peace by His daily intercession. What saint alive does not sometimes offend God and cause the fury of His anger to rise up in His face? Now when the case is thus, that we offend God and are ready to break His peace, then Jesus Christ stands up as an intercessor and speaks to God the Father on our behalf. And it is His request that God would lay aside His anger and that He would smile upon His people again. Therefore, in Scripture, Christ is called our atonement to make peace, and He is called our Advocate to purchase peace. When we break our peace, Christ pleads our case and makes up this peace again by His intercession, 1 John 3:7.

USE 1. To make some application of this, first, by way of inference, see here to what coast we must trade for this pearl. See where we must go for this spiritual peace that is our consolation in life and death. Go to Christ for it: "That in Me ye might have peace."

Cyprian said, "Peace is in Christ as sap is in the root of the vine, as water is in the springs." "That in Me ye might have peace," said Christ. This blessed peace that Christ gives is worth going to Him for; it is superior to all other peace. Peace in a kingdom is very desirable;

peace is everyone's vote. Peace is the very quintessence
of earthly blessings, to sit quietly under our vines and
fig trees. Surely better, a great deal better, is the sounding of the lute and the violin than the roaring of the
cannon. See what a sweet promise God makes, Isaiah
2:4. He will break their swords into plowshares. All
shall be peace. But what is this peace to the peace
Christ gives to His people that is sacred? This peace
our Savior gives has these two properties or qualifica-
tions: it is an emboldening peace and it is a lasting
peace.

It is an emboldening peace. Friends that are at
peace use a kind of freedom and boldness one with
another. So we, having peace through Christ's blood
conveyed by His Spirit, may be bold to make use of
God's promises. There is never a promise in the Bible
but a believer may pluck a leaf from, and be at peace
with God through Christ. We may now use a holy
boldness in prayer. We may come to God as children to
their father, Hebrews 4:16. Let us come with boldness
to the throne of grace. God is our Father, and He, being at peace with us, will not deny anything that may
conduce to our real good. This may make us come
with boldness to the mercy seat. That's the first prop-
erty. It is an emboldening peace.

Christ's peace, as it is an emboldening peace, so it
is also a lasting peace. Here is a peace that will hold.
All earthly peace, to speak properly, is a truce rather
than a peace. A truce is but for a small time and it
ends, yea, but this peace that Christ gives is forever.
Once in Christ and ever in Christ. Once justified and
ever justified. Here is a lasting peace. Isaiah 54:10:
"The covenant of my peace shall not be removed, saith

the Lord." The peace of a believer is but begun here in this life; it is perfected in the kingdom of heaven. Isaiah 57:2: "He shall enter into peace." Here is a godly man's privilege. When he dies, he dies in peace; and as soon as he is dead he enters into peace. That is, he shall go to the Jerusalem above, that city of peace. Here the saints' peace is but begun; it is but in the seed, there it shall be in the flower. Here it is but in its infancy; there it shall be in its full growth. That's the first. See to what coast you must trade for this peace. Go to Christ for it. "That in Me ye might have peace."

Second, see what a sad condition all wicked men are in who live and die in their sins. They have nothing to do with peace. What! Shall they have peace who make war with heaven and persecute Christ in His members? Shall they have peace who deride and grieve the Spirit of God, whose very office it is to drop peace into the conscience? What, a sinner to have peace? 2 Kings 9:22: "What peace, so long as the whoredoms of thy mother Jezebel and her witchcrafts are so many!" A wicked man is a worker of iniquity. As a man works at his shop, so he works at the trade of sin; and what has he to do with peace? And how deplorable is his case!

If a foreign enemy should come, sinners would be in a storm and have nowhere to put in for harbor. It is a very sad thing to be in Saul's condition with the Philistines upon him and God departed from him. It is a very sad thing to have fightings without and fears within, to have the bullets shooting against the ship and the ship leaking within. Isaiah 57:21: "There is no peace to the wicked, saith my God." And if God says it, he knows it to be true.

The wicked may perhaps delude themselves and presume that, though they go on in sin, they shall have peace. But to undeceive them, turn to one Scripture, Deuteronomy 29:19-20: "And it come to pass when he heareth the words of this curse, that he blesses himself in his heart, saying, I shall have peace, though I walk in the imagination of mine heart. . . . The Lord will not spare him, but then the anger of the Lord and His jealousy shall smoke against that man."

One may as well think to suck health out of poison as to suck peace out of sin. Sinners may be quiet or rather secure for the present, but it will be bitterness in the end as in 2 Samuel 26. Guilt will sooner or later raise a storm, said Chrysostom. Sin will conjure up the winds and storms into the conscience.

I have sometimes thought it is with sin as it is with poison. There are some sorts of poison that will lie a great while in the body and not work, but at last it wrings and tortures the bowels—a fit resemblance of sin. Men drink this poison, and they may be quiet a while, but at last, especially at death, then it begins to work and then the poison begins to touch the conscience.

The great God of heaven and earth has set up His standard and proclaimed open war against every impenitent sinner. And it will not be long, if men go on in sin, before God's cannon bullets will begin to fly. God's wrath may seem like a sleeping lion, but this lion will awake and roar and tear his prey. I will only say this. I confess God may bear long with wicked men and leave them alone. He may bear long with them in respect of punishment when He does not remit the sin. But it will be sad with the sinner at last, a sad hour at death. The body and soul must part, and Christ and the soul must part. "There is no peace to the wicked, saith my God." Can they have peace who strike against the crown and dignity of heaven, who make war with Christ, God, and heaven?

USE 2. OF TRIAL.
Let us then search and examine. Have we this secret and sweet peace in our souls flowing from the Lord Jesus? You may know it these three ways, and they are three sure notes that will never fail.
1. *Such as have Christ's peace in their souls are engrafted into Christ.* They are one with Christ. Mark the words of the text, "In Me ye shall have peace." First, we must be *in* Christ before we can have peace *from* Christ. "In Me." Then comes peace. The graft or branch must first be inoculated into the tree before it receives sap and influence from the tree. We must by faith be inoculated into Christ before we can receive of His fullness.

The wicked may presume to have peace, and that they shall have peace, and yet they are not acquainted with Christ. Do they think ever to have an interest in Christ's peace who have no interest in Christ's person? It cannot be. A Christless soul has no more claim to Christ's peace than a woman can lay claim to a man's estate who was never married to him. "In Me," said Christ. First you must be in Christ and then you shall have peace from Christ, sacred peace. It is a legacy that Christ bequeaths. He gives this legacy not to strangers but to His friends, such as are united to Him.

The pipe must first be laid to the spring before it receives water from the spring. So we must first by faith be united to Christ, laid to this spring by faith, before we can receive the sweet influences of peace from him.

2. *Wherever Christ gives peace to any soul, there He always sets up His governing scepter to bear sway in that soul.* A pregnant Scripture for this is Isaiah 9:7, "Of His government and peace there shall be no end." There must be Christ's government set up in the soul before there is peace. Whenever the Lord Jesus comes with an olive branch of peace in His mouth, He always comes with a scepter in His hand. A parallel Scripture for this is Zechariah 6:13. It is a promise of Christ: "He shall sit and rule, and He shall be a priest upon the throne." Observe, Christ as a priest makes peace, but He will be a priest upon the throne. That is, He will bring the heart, where He gives peace, into a full subjection to His laws. He will be a priest upon His throne.

Now, let us examine. Have we given subjection to Christ Jesus? Do we submit to His blessed laws? Does Christ sit and rule in our hearts as a priest upon His throne? Then all is well. There are many people who would have Christ to speak peace to them, but they will not suffer Him to rule. They would have His olive branch but they will not endure His scepter.

3. *If Christ has given us this blessed peace, then we shall know it by this: He has made us to be of a meek, quiet, and peaceable disposition.* Wherever Christ gives His peace, He makes the heart to be peaceable. Isaiah 11:6: "The wolf shall dwell with the lamb; the leopard shall lie down with the kid." That is, after grace is brought into a man's heart, and Christ has given him peace, this man becomes of a peaceable and quiet disposition. Now, "the wolf shall dwell with the lamb." The fierceness of the wolf shall be turned into the meekness of the lamb.

Bernard, that good man, was a man of a peaceable
spirit. And any time someone fell out with him he
would say, "I will be at peace with you, though you go
on in trouble." Such turbulent spirits that are troublers
of the common peace are like the salamander that lives
in the fire of broils and of contention; and they love to
live in this fire.

Surely, where Christ gives this peace, it makes men
of a peaceable spirit. It turns the briar into a myrtle
tree. So by this we may know whether Christ has given
us this peace or not.

USE 3. And here I will turn myself to such as are
acquainted with Christ and this blessed peace.

First, have you this blessed peace from Christ?
Then be not overly troubled about the afflictions and
encumbrances that are incidental to this present life. It
is true, our lives are full of vicissitudes and troubles. It
will be so. He who does not expect some trouble must
go out of the world. Fear and grief are the two constant
companions of man's life. You may as well separate
weight from lead or moisture from the air as trouble
from the life of man. Does not the text say, "In the
world you shall have tribulation"?

But here is that which may sweeten the troubles of
God's people. Christ gives peace. Here is an antidote
against your fears and troubles. And there is no antidote like a Scripture antidote. Christ said, "That in Me
ye might have peace." This is a glorious peace indeed.
It is a peace that will hold out in a storm and tempest.
It turns a prison into a paradise. It turns our mourning
into music. It turns our sighs into songs and triumphs.
That holy man dated his letter thus: "Written from the

pleasant garden of the lion prison."

David was Christ-prepared. And therefore the times were never so stormy. He would lie down in peace. Psalm 4:8: "I will lay me down in peace." It was a very tempestuous time. David was fleeing from his son Absalom. Now, said David, "I will lay me down in peace." I will take a nap and sleep sweetly upon this good pillow of conscience. David was in danger of losing two jewels at once, but there was a third jewel he could not lose, and that was a good conscience.

I read of one who had a precious stone, and it was of such brightness that it made it be like the ark when it was tossing upon the water. Let me allude to it. If Jesus Christ has given us this peace, this will give light to the soul when the clouds gather and you are tossing upon the waters of affliction.

Second, if Christ has given you a well-grounded peace, oh! be thankful for this great gift. No rhetoric, no tongue of angels can set it forth in all its glory. Peace of soul makes harmony in a Christian. Though there are never so many discouragements in the world, yet he enjoys harmony in his own soul. This inward peace is the best music. That you may be thankful for this peace, consider how sad it is to lack this peace because this is the contrary of it.

I argue thus:

If the devil and horror of conscience are so dreadful, then certainly inward peace of conscience flowing from Christ must be very sweet. To have conscience vex and fury is, as it is well-called, a sharp fury. Spira had that inward horror of soul when he had sinned so that he died with the fear and terror of hell in his soul. He thought judgment less than that. Now if the sting of conscience is so bitter, then the peace of conscience must be sweet.

Has God set your soul, which was once like a troublesome sea, now to be calm and peaceful? Oh! then sound your harp and violin. Admire this God; sing forth praises and acclamations unto Christ, this blessed Prince of Peace.

Last, if Christ has spoken peace, if He has dropped this blessed peace into your souls, then let me beseech you that you would be careful not to lose this jewel. Labor to preserve this peace in your souls. Preserve your peace as you would preserve your lives.

And to that end:

1. If you would preserve your peace, take heed of relapses. They are dangerous. Do not tamper any more with sin. Dare not to feed sin in a corner. Sin is the peace-breaker. Psalm 85:8: "The Lord will speak peace to His people." But what follows? "But let them not return again to folly." Let them not return again to their sins any more. There is a great deal of folly in our relapsing from a strict and holy life.

2. Would you preserve this jewel in your bosoms, this blessed peace? Then make up your accounts with God daily. Often reckoning keeps God and conscience friends. Psalm 4:4: "Commune with your own hearts." That is, call yourselves to an account. Make up your account, make them even, see how things stand between God and your souls. Observe whether your affections are lively. Examine your evidences and see if there is no decay in your graces, no loss of first love. Oh! keep the reckoning even between God and you. That's the way to keep your peace.

3. Walk closely with God every day. Live as under

the continual inspection of God's omniscient eye. Live
holily. Peace and purity go together. The way to preserve our peace is to preserve our integrity. Oh! keep
your constant hours every day with God. Turn your
closets into temples. Search the Scriptures. The two
Testaments are the two lips by which God has spoken.
Love the Word. Love prayer. Love the Sabbath. Psalm
119:165: "Great peace have they that love Thy law."

Thus you may sweetly enjoy yourselves, and this
jewel of peace will be preserved in your bosoms.

Kiss the Son

"Kiss the Son, lest He be angry, and ye perish in the way, when His wrath is kindled but a little. Blessed are all they that put their trust in Him." Psalm 2:12

In the beginning of this Psalm, holy David shows us how all the powers and gallantry of the world rage and confederate against the Lord and His anointed, that is, Christ. Verse 2: "Rulers take counsel against the Lord and His anointed." That power which He put into their hands they employ against Him, but their attempt is in vain. In the first verse, "The people imagine a vain thing," as if the holy Psalmist had said, "The Lord will have a church in spite of earth and hell." Matthew 16:18: "The gates of hell shall not prevail against it"; that is, neither the power of hell nor the policy of hell shall prevail against His Church. Neither the serpent's subtlety nor yet the dragon's fierceness shall prevail against it.

We read that the ship in the gospel was tossed on the waves but was not overwhelmed because Christ was in it. Christ is in the ship of His Church, and the more opposition is made against the Church of God, the more it increases. It grows by opposition, Exodus 1:12. "The more they were afflicted the more they multiplied," said Chrysostom. It is just like the torch—the more it is beaten the more it flames. Religion is that phoenix that is always flourishing in the ashes of martyrs. Therefore, let the great ones conspire and take counsel against the Lord and His Christ; they imagine a vain thing.

In the 4th verse we read that when the wicked sit plotting, God smiles at them: "He that sits in the heavens shall laugh at them." God laughs to see men's folly, to see poor, weak clay go to take head and strive with the potter. But let the wicked remember that God is never more angry with them than when He laughs. He will speak to them in a fair language, as you may read in verse 5. After His laughing, then He shall speak to them in His wrath. And what does He say? Verse 6: "Yet have I set My King upon My holy hill of Zion." In spite of all the powers of darkness, Jesus Christ shall have a throne to sit upon among His people. "I have set My King," that is, I have anointed Christ to be King and have poured on Him the ointment of grace and gladness. I will have My Son to reign, and such as will not bow to His golden scepter shall be broken with His iron rod, verse 9.

Then, after this, the Psalmist makes the inference. Before he had been making the doctrine to kings and the great ones of the world. Now he makes the use in verse 10: "Be wise now therefore, O ye kings! Be instructed, ye judges of the earth. Serve the Lord with fear." As if he had said, "Come at last to your wits; don't stand out any longer in contest with God and His Son, Jesus Christ. But rather bow to Him; throw your crowns at His feet; make your peace with Him. Serve the Lord with fear." So the text ushers in. And it is a part of the good counsel the Holy Ghost gives, "Kiss

the Son, lest He be angry, and ye perish in the way."
Kissing the Son denotes two things:
First, adoration. It was an ancient custom to kiss the son when they admired him, Job 31:27. So Jerome and others read it, "Admire the Son." Adoration is a crown jewel, proper to Christ and to His crown. Admire the Son, that's the first thing.
Second, kissing the Son denotes subjection. So we find in 1 Samuel 10:1. Samuel kissed Saul when he anointed him king. He kissed him in token of homage and subjection to him. So that's the meaning of the text: Kiss the Son, that is, admire Him and be subject to Him.
The text then falls into these two parts:
First, here's a duty: Kiss the Son.
Second, the reason of it, and that is very cogent: Lest He be angry.
So here are two propositions that result from the words. I shall only speak to the first, and draw the other in the application.
DOCTRINE 1. Jesus Christ is the Son of God.
DOCTRINE 2. It is a great point of prudence to highly value and love, to kiss and admire, this blessed Son of God.

DOCTRINE 1. Jesus Christ is the Son of God. "Kiss the Son." He is the Son of God, not by creation, as the angels are said to be His sons, but He is His Son by eternal generation. Hebrews 1:3: "Who being the brightness of His glory, and the express image of His person." Observe, Jesus Christ is the Son of God, for He is the brightness of His Father's glory. You know that the brightness that issues from the sun is of the

same nature with the sun in the firmament. So Jesus
Christ is the brightness of His Father; He is of the same
nature with His Father as the beams are of the same
nature with the sun. Therefore, Christ says, John 14:9,
"He that hath seen Me hath seen My Father."

Again, observe that Christ is called the brightness
of His Father's glory. The glory of the sun in the firmament lies in the brightness of it. So the incomparable glory of the Father most shines in Jesus Christ. He
is the brightness of His Father's glory. And this is
enough to demonstrate to us that Christ is the very Son
of God. And as Christ is the Son of God, so He is a
royal Son. He is a Son as He is a King. "I have set My
King upon My holy hill of Zion," Psalm 2:6. Jesus
Christ is said in Scripture to be the "Prince of the kings
of the earth," Revelation 1:5. All kings hold their
crowns by immediate tenor from Jesus Christ. Proverbs
8:15: "By Me princes reign." So Christ is a royal Son.
He is such a Son that He is a King. Indeed, He has the
titles given to Him of a King.

He is called high and mighty, Isaiah 9:6, "the
mighty God."

As He is a King, He has His ensigns of royalty. He
has His sword, Psalm 49:3. He has His scepter in His
hand, Hebrews 1:8.

Again, as Christ is King, He has His royal preroga-
tive. For instance, He has power to make laws. He has
power to pardon offenders, which are jewels belonging
to the crowns of princes.

Again, He has His subjects, and they are the most
noble and excellent subjects in the world, and that in a
threefold respect:

First, all Christ's subjects are made free, John 18:36.

His subjects fear Him from an ingenuous principle of
love. They do not serve Christ out of constraint but out
of choice. They are of a free, noble spirit.
Second, Christ's subjects have the Spirit of the living God in them. They have the indwelling of the Holy
Ghost, 2 Timothy 1:14.
Third, all Christ's subjects are of the royal blood of
heaven. They are kings, Revelation 1:8. Thus you see
that Christ is a Son, He is a King, and He has His subjects.
Christ as King has His dominions. There are some
princes who have titles, but they do not have dominions. But Christ has dominions as well as titles of
honor. He has lands belonging to His crown. Christ's
dominions are famous for three things:
First, they are large dominions. God has given Him
as King the uttermost parts of the earth for His possession. His kingdom reaches all over the world.
Second, Christ's dominion is famous for its spirituality. The Lord Jesus sets up His throne and kingdom
where no other king can. He rules the hearts of men;
He gives laws in their consciences; He binds their souls
by His laws. Here is the spirituality of His kingdom.
Third, here is the eternity of His kingdom. "Thy
throne, O God, is forever and ever," Hebrews 1:8.
What king can say so? It's true, He has many heirs, for
all believers are His heirs, yet He has no successors.
Earthly crowns fade away and tumble in the dirt, as do
those who wear them. Does the crown endure to all
generations? No, there is a worm that feeds in this
gold. But Christ's throne endures forever. As the Lord
Jesus has the largest possessions, for so He has, they
shall endure forever and ever.

And thus much for the doctrinal part. Jesus Christ
is the Son of God, the brightness of His glory. And He
is a royal Son. He is so a Son as He is a King. Now to
make some application.

USE 1. OF INFERENCE.

Is Jesus Christ the Son of God? A King full of glory
and majesty? Then it informs us this much: All matters
of fact must be brought before this Son of God. It is
the Son of God, His royal Son, by whom all princes
reign. Learn from hence that all matter of fact must be
brought before this Son. Christ has the power of life
and death in His hand. John 5:22: "The Father hath
committed all judgment (all government) to the Son."

That blessed Lord Jesus who once had a reed put
into His hand by way of scorn and contempt shall
shortly have a royal scepter put into His hand as some
great king. That Jesus who once hung on the cross
shall shortly sit as Judge upon the bench. God has
committed all judgment to the Son. The whole world
must shortly come before the Son. That's the last and
great assize from whence there is no appeal. This
blessed Son of God is fitly qualified to be the Judge of
the world in respect of these two things.

1. Jesus Christ has wisdom to understand all causes.
He is the Son of God. He is God, and therefore will
search to the bottom of all causes. Therefore He is described with seven eyes to denote His omniscience to
judge things. Jesus Christ weighs the spirits of men, as
it were, in a balance, Job 16:2. He is said to weigh the
spirit. Christ not only judges matter of fact, but He
judges men's hearts. Many men's actions may seem in
this world to be good, but their hearts are not good, 2

Chronicles 25:2. Now Christ, this great Judge, has this
touchstone to try the heart.

2. Jesus Christ has not only wisdom, but He has
strength too whereby He is able to be avenged upon all
His enemies. Therefore in Scripture it is remarkable
that Christ's seven eyes are said to be upon one stone.
Seven eyes upon one stone denote the infinite strength
of Christ, the power and mighty strength of Christ. As
Christ has His balance, so He has His sword to cut off
offenders. He can easily strike through the loins of His
enemies, Psalm 110. Thus the Son of God, this royal
Son, is to be Judge, and all causes and all matters will
be brought before His judgment seat. Christ's court is
the highest court of judicature. If men are once cast
there, there is no appeal to any other court.

USE 2. OF EXHORTATION.

A second use I would make of this point is a use of
exhortation, and it has three or four branches in it:

First, if Jesus Christ is the Son of God, so full of
glory and majesty, and shall sit upon the bench of judicature, then let all great ones take heed how they employ their power against Jesus Christ. It is Christ who
gives them their power. "By Me," said Christ, "princes
reign," Proverbs 8:15. Power and sovereignty are talents that Christ entrusts men with; and He will shortly
call them to account for what they have done with this
talent. And if it is found that they have employed this
talent against Jesus Christ, O what a dismal account will
they have to make! Christ is set up to be a King, and
whoever opposes Christ in His kingly office, who says,
"We will not have this man to reign over us," will find
that Christ will be too hard for them.

For men to lift themselves up against Christ is as if a little child should go to fight with an archangel. Isaiah 8:9: "Associate yourselves, O ye people, and ye shall be broken in pieces." This is the voice of God's church speaking to its enemies. The church of God, having such a champion on her side as the Lord Christ is, exults over all her enemies.

Second, if Jesus Christ is the Son of God, then let us labor, all of us, to become one with Christ. Then we also shall be the sons of God. Christ makes all the saints to become sons of God, Romans 8:17-18. Christ is a Son by eternal generation, and believers are His sons by adoption. David thought it a great honor to be son-in-law to a king, 1 Samuel 18:18. What an infinite honor to be the sons of the most high God! As Christ is the Son of God, so grace makes us to be the sons of God. God accounts all His sons to be honorable, and they must be so.

Such honor have all His saints, for they are born of God and fetch their pedigree from heaven. Isaiah 43:4: "Since thou wast precious in My sight, thou hast been honorable." Their tears are put into God's own bottle. He gives the saints a partnership with Christ in His glory. God lays up a portion for all His sons. He gives them a kingdom when they die. Luke 12:32, "It is My Father's good pleasure to give you the kingdom." O! Who would not labor for grace? As Christ is the Son of God, so grace makes us to become the sons of God. And, being sons, we are heirs to all God's promises. The promises are a cabinet of jewels, and God has bestowed this cabinet upon His sons. Therefore saints are called heirs of the promises, Hebrews 6:17, and heirs of eternal life, Titus 3:7.

O you saints of God! Think of this! If you are sons, why, though you may lose and suffer the spoiling of your goods, as the primitive saints did, Hebrews 10:34, yet you shall not lose your portion; for your heavenly Father will keep a portion for you in His kingdom.

Third, if Christ is the Son of God, then let us all be willing to hear Christ's voice when He speaks to us. This I ground upon that Scripture in Matthew 17:5, "This is My beloved Son, hear Him." This is the inference that God Himself makes. When Jesus Christ calls for us in His Word to believe and repent, He is said to speak from heaven to us. O then let us hear the Son! God knows how long we shall hear the Son speaking to us. Shall we hearken to a lust? Shall we hearken to a temptation? Shall we hear the serpent's voice, and shall we not hear the Son's voice? O let us not despise the voice of the Son of God!

If God should speak to us now as He did to the people when He gave the Law with thundering and earthquakes, then we would tremble as they did. Exodus 20:18-19: "Let not the Lord speak to us, lest we die." But when God speaks to us, Hebrews 1:2, with a still, small voice of the gospel; when God woos and beseeches us by His Son, 2 Corinthians 5:19; "Turn ye, turn ye; why will ye die?" Ezekiel 18:31-32; "Hear, and your souls shall live," Isaiah 55:2—shall we not now hear the voice of the Son of God? If we will not hear Christ's first voice—"Come unto Me, you that are weary and heavy laden," Matthew 11:28—we shall never hear Christ's second voice: "Come to Me, ye blessed," Luke 25:34.

Fourth, which is the main thing, if Christ is the Son of God, a king full of glory and majesty, as you have

heard, then take the counsel in the text: "Kiss the Son, lest He be angry." Kiss Christ, this blessed Son of God, with a threefold kiss. Kiss Him:
1. With a kiss of faith.
2. With a kiss of love.
3. With a kiss of obedience.

1. *Kiss Christ the Son of God with a kiss of faith.* This is indeed to kiss Him, when we believe in Him. So it follows in the words of the text, "Blessed are they that put their trust in Him," to believe and confide in His merit. This believing kiss is that which Christ looks for to affect our thoughts and confidence in the merit of the Son of God. This kiss of faith, said Austin, is, as it were, to set foot in heaven. When we begin to believe, we have got one foot in heaven. It is the main thing in the gospel to believe in the Son. Acts 13:39: "By Him all that believe are justified." We may believe sometimes when we don't know we believe. As there may be life when there is no lively sense, so in faith, we may have faith when we don't know it. I am not justified because I believe, but because I know I believe. This kiss of faith, believing in Christ, is the best kiss we can give to Christ. This He takes most kindly at our hands. For when we believe, then we honor the Son as we honor the Father. It sets the crown upon the head of Christ.

Now, because there is so much weight lying upon this believing in the Son of God, I shall show you, first, what it is to believe in Him. It is not only an assent that Jesus Christ is the true Messiah, but there must be a fiducial encumbency, a leaning on Christ as the spouse did in Song of Solomon 8:5: "Who is this that comes leaning on her beloved?" All other pillows will break but this one. This pillow you can never lean too hard upon. Jesus Christ is a golden pillow that bears all that is laid upon Him. This believing in Christ is a catching hold of His merit. One who is ready to drown catches hold of the bow or twig to keep him from sinking. O! Nothing will keep us from eternally sinking in the sea of God's wrath but catching hold of Jesus Christ. Believing is a holy adventure upon Christ. Queen Esther adventured into the presence of the king. "If I perish, I perish," said she. This is the language of faith: "If I perish, I perish." Who ever perished believing?

Second, this kissing of Christ by faith is hard. It is not an easy matter. It is easy to profess this Son of God, but it is not easy to kiss this Son. That which makes this work of believing hard lies in these two things:

It is hard because man has set up the idol of self-righteousness. He is apt to think he has something of his own growth in him—righteousness of his own, his prayers, his tears, his alms. He would make a Christ of them. Instead of kissing the Son, he idolizes himself. Man is a proud piece of flesh. He would see some worthiness in himself. He would give part to himself and part to Christ. He is loath to be beholden to grace only. He would grow upon his own root and not be grafted upon the stock of Christ's righteousness. Romans 10:3: "Going about to establish a righteousness of their own, they have not submitted themselves to the righteousness of God." O! It's wonderful to see a proud sinner humbled, to see him go out of himself to Christ for righteousness. That's the first thing.

The second thing that makes this work of believing so hard is that believing is a work above the power of

nature to produce. It is a work of supernatural infus-
ing, John 6:29. Faith is called the work of God. It's the
work of God to believe. Faith is a new creation. The
creation of the world is called the work of God's finger,
but the creation of faith is called the work of God's
arm. The Lord sets all His strength to work. It is called
"the exceeding greatness of His power," Ephesians
1:20. Surely to raise Christ from the dead required a
great power. He had a heavy gravestone laid upon
Him, the sins of the whole world. Why, the same power
God puts forth in the producing of faith in the soul. So
that this kissing of Christ by faith is not as easy as most
imagine.

The third aspect of believing in Christ is that wherever this blessed work of faith is, it has some virtue that
goes along with it. It has a refining, consecrating
virtue. The kiss of faith is a holy kiss; it purifies the
heart and makes it holy, Acts 15:9. Faith is in the heart
as fire among metal. It purifies it and takes away the
dross. A kiss of faith has the same virtue as the touch-
ing of Christ by faith. The woman touched the hem of
Christ's garment by faith, and immediately she received healing virtue from that touch, Mark 5:34. Thus
faith touches Christ and heals. True faith draws a sanctifying and a mortifying virtue from the Lord Jesus.
Justifying faith may be called a faith of spiritual miracles, for it removes mountains of sins and throws them
into Christ's blood.

Whoever kisses the Son by faith is presently made
holy. The truth is, faith argues a man to holiness. It
falls to reasoning with him: "O my soul! Has Christ
done so much for me? Has He forgiven me so many
debts? Has He purchased such rich mercy in His

blood? And will you abuse the love of so dear a friend? Will you make the wounds of your dear Savior to bleed afresh? Is this to kiss the Son? O my soul! How should you give up yourself to Christ in holiness!"

And then faith reasons: "If your tears will wash Christ's feet, will you not pour them out? If your estate is a precious ointment, will you not pour out this ointment upon part of Christ's body and relieve His members?"

Now the soul cannot withstand these melting reasons, but immediately yields to all. Faith is a holy gift; it consecrates the heart wherever it comes.

Fourth, to kiss the Son by faith is the most excellent way of worshipping Him. There's nothing like believing. Let me set forth a little to you the excellency of faith.

This is the main thing the Scripture holds forth and presses you to. If one should ask why the Scriptures were written, the answer is to point us to Christ the true Messiah, and that we should embrace him by faith. John 20:31: "These things are written that you might believe that Jesus is the Christ, the Son of God, and that believing you might have life through His name." This is the marrow of the gospel. It's the sovereign cordial of a fainting soul, that by believing on the Lord Jesus Christ he may be saved.

This blessed believing, kissing the Son by faith, is the most excellent of graces. It excels all others, even as gold among metals. Every grace is very lovely, but this of faith excels them all.

Consider these five particulars:

Faith is the uniting grace; therefore this grace excels. Other graces conform us to Christ but faith unites us to Christ; it espouses us to Him. Other graces make us *like* Christ, but faith makes us one *with* Christ. Other graces make us pictures of Christ but faith makes us branches of Christ.

Faith is the vital grace. By kissing Christ we fetch life from Him. "The just shall live by faith," Habakkuk 2:4. By believing we fetch life from Christ. "I live by the faith of the Son of God," said the Apostle, Galatians 2:20. As the arm lives by drawing life from the heart, so faith lives by drawing life and strength from Christ. Other graces are useful but faith is vital.

Faith is the justifying grace; therefore it is most excellent. Romans 5:1: "Being justified by faith." It is not repentance that justifies, nor self-denial, but faith. Faith is the most proper grace of all to justify a sinner, for the hand is more fit to receive the food than the eye. So faith is the most proper to justify because, when we believe, we don't give anything to Christ, but we fetch something from Him.

Faith is a world-conquering grace. 1 John 5:4: "This is the victory over the world, even our faith." Faith overcomes all the allurements of the world, the riches of the world, the delights of the world, and it does it by showing the soul a better world than this is. Faith gives it a prospect of prosperity. It carries a believer to the Mount of Transfiguration. It makes him see things that are not seen by the eye of sense, Hebrews 12:1. Faith leads the soul to Christ the bright morning star. It gives the soul a view of Him, and He is known in the embroidered robes of His glory. Faith shows a man a kingdom. It trades above the moon, and when once a soul has a shadow of these things, it despises all the pleasures of this world.

Last, faith is a suffering grace. It enables us to wade
through the deep waters of affliction. Hebrews 11:25:
"By faith Moses chose rather to suffer affliction with
the people of God than to enjoy the pleasure of sin for
a season." Faith is a furnace grace; it gives the soul a
right notion of suffering. What is this suffering? Faith
says it is but a light affliction, 2 Corinthians 4:17-18.
The cross is light in comparison to the cross which
Christ conformed to. The cross is light in comparison
to the weight of glory, and thus faith makes the soul go
through affliction.

This kissing of Christ by faith pleases God more
than anything we can do besides. It is better than to
give God rivers of oil; it is better than sacrifice. It is
faith that pleases God. This is the savory meat which
God loves to taste. And the reason why believing is so
pleasing to God is that, by believing, we bring a righteousness into God's presence which is perfectly meritorious. We don't bring the righteousness of Adam
into court, or the righteousness of angels, but we bring
the righteousness of God. And this is that which makes
believing so pleasing to God.

If then to kiss Christ by faith is the great work under the gospel, why then, let us labor to kiss the Son of
God by believing in Him and putting and placing our
full hope in Him. That's the first thing: Kiss Him with a
kiss of faith.

2. *We must kiss the Son of God with a kiss of love.*
Indeed, Christ is the wonder of beauty. He is nothing
but love. God is love, 1 John 4:8. Christ has that
majesty in Him which may draw reverence, and He has
that mercy in Him that may draw love to Him. The

Lord Jesus is a whole paradise of delight. Why then, kiss Him with a kiss of love. Let it be a sincere love. 1 Corinthians 16:21: "Grace be with them that love the Lord Jesus in sincerity and truth."

Don't kiss Him with a Judas kiss to betray Him, but love Him sincerely; that is, love His person more than jewels. Love Christ more for what He is than for what He has; and then love Christ with a superlative love, a love above all things whatsoever. Christ has loved you more than others, you who are believers. He has loved you with such a love that He does not bestow upon the wicked. You have electing love, you have adopting love. Let your love to Christ be such a love that none else but Christ may be a sharer. That is, give Christ a love that is joined with adoration. Don't only kiss Christ with your lips, but worship Him in your hearts. That's the second point: Kiss Christ with a kiss of love. He deserves your love most, and He deserves your love best.

3. *Kiss Christ with a kiss of obedience.* This is to kiss Christ, when we submit to Him, when we obey His laws, when we are under His jurisdiction. There are many in the world who give Christ a complementary kiss. They seem devout and jealous; they bow and cringe. O but they don't obey the Son! They kiss Christ as their Savior but they will not submit to Him as their Prince. The truth is, they would have Christ and their lusts together. They would embrace His promises but they will not obey His commands. O kiss the Son with a kiss of subjection!

We should be like the needle that points the way which the loadstone draws. Those who will not have Christ's laws to rule them shall never have Christ's blood to save them.

Now, to persuade you to kiss the Lord Jesus with a kiss of obedience, consider these two things:

The first is in the text: "lest He be angry." Anger is not in Christ as a passion, but anger is said to be in Christ as a displeasure in Him. And His punishing of offenders is the effect of His displeasure. "Who knows the power of His anger?" O therefore, "kiss the Son lest He be angry"! See that place in Revelation 6:15: "The kings of the earth, the great men hid themselves in the dens, and in the rocks of the mountains; and said to the rocks and the mountains, Fall on us, and hide us from the face of Him that sits on the throne, and from the wrath of the Lamb." Now the Lamb of God is turned into a lion, and therefore they cry out to the rocks, "O hide us from the wrath of the Lamb!"

He who has no part in the blood of the Lamb will have a part in the wrath of the Lamb. If you will not kiss the Son and lie down at His feet and submit to Him, then you must fall into His hands. And the Apostle said, "It is a fearful thing to fall into the hands of the living God," Hebrews 10:31. It is good to fall into His hands when He is a friend. O but it's sad to fall into His hands when He is an adversary! God is the sweetest friend but He is the sourest enemy. When but one spark of God's wrath lights upon a man it is so terrible; what is it, then, to have the whole furnace of His wrath! How easily can the Lord Jesus crumble us to dust? He can unpin the whole world! O then "kiss the Son lest He be angry."

The mountains quake at His presence, and will not the sinner's heart quake? Perhaps you think this Lion is not as fierce as He is painted. Look into one

Scripture, Ezekiel 22:14: "Can thine heart endure, or can thine hand be strong in the day that I shall deal with thee?"

If we kiss the Son by believing in Him and obeying Him, Christ will answer love with love. He will smile upon us. He will kiss us with the kisses of His mouth. Song of Solomon 1:8: "Let Him kiss me with the kisses of His mouth; for His love is better than wine." Christ will lay us forever in His bosom, and if we give Him a kiss of love, He will give us a crown of life, Revelation 2.

THE LAST USE.

Here is a word of terror to wicked men. Instead of kissing the Son, they disobey Him, dishonor Him, vex His Spirit, and do all they can to spite Him. They take counsel against the Lord and His anointed. Are there not many who do all they can to overturn Christ's interests? They would stop the conduit pipes that transmit the water of life. Revelation 17:14: "They shall make war with the Lamb, and the Lamb shall overcome them." Christ will get the victory. He will come off as Conqueror. Jesus Christ will lay His saints in His bosom, but He will put His enemies under His feet. Psalm 110:1: "I will make Mine enemies My footstool." Those who will not be ruled by Christ's royal scepter, His scepter of grace, shall be broken by His rod of iron. In short, all those who oppose Christ shall be as so many ripe clusters of grapes to be cast into the great winepress of God's wrath, and to be trodden by the Son of God till their blood squeezes out. The Lord Jesus shoots His arrows very deep into the very hearts of His enemies, Psalm 54:5. His arrows are sharp in the hearts of His enemies. The Persians dip their arrows in poison to kill more mortally. So Jesus Christ shoots His arrows of poison; and because they cannot endure the wrath of the Lamb all at once, they will be enduring it to eternity. So, therefore, here is terror to all those who do not kiss the Son.

Till My Change Comes

"All the days of my appointed time will I wait till my change comes." Job 14:14

This book relates the history of Job's sufferings. He was a tall cedar in grace, yet this cedar grew in a valley of tears. Religion gives no charter of exemption from trouble. Job's trials were so sharp that he began to grow weary of life and was willing to have a writ of ease to have his pass and be gone. Job 14:13: "O, that Thou wouldest hide me in the grave!" This holy man was much afflicted in his meditations of his end. He walked among the tombs and walked into his grave before it was dug, and by frequent thoughts labored to make death familiar to him. "All the days of my appointed time will I wait till my change comes."

The text is a large field. I shall only, as I pass along, pluck some few ears of corn.

In the words there are three general parts observable:

1. A description of life: "all my days."

2. The determination of life: "my appointed time."

3. A holy resolution: "I will wait till my change comes."

1. I begin with the first. Here is a description of life: "all my days."

DOCTRINE. Job does not measure his life by years but by days.

82

Nay, he calls life a day in verse 6 of this chapter. Man's life very much resembles a day in four respects.

1. Life is like a day for the shortness of it. Men dream of a long life, said Austin. Men think of such a thing as an earthly eternity, but it is a short day. Infancy is a daybreak; youth is sunrise; full growth is the sun in its meridian; old age is sunset; sickness is evening, and then comes the night of death. Life is a day, and is it so short? Is it but a day? Why do we then rather lose time than live it?

2. Life is like a day for the vicissitudes that are in it. A day has much alteration and change of weather. The morning that shows bright and clear may at noon show black clouds and rain. One part of the day is calm and serene; the other part of it is blusterous and windy. Such is our life. It is like a day. What change of weather is there in man's life? What sudden alterations fall out? Sometimes health, sometimes sickness, sometimes prosperity, and sometimes adversity. Here is change of wealth. Sometimes we see the white lily of peace; sometimes again the red rose of a bloody war appears. Here is change of weather.

3. Life is a day for labor. The day is the time for working, Psalm 104:23. The sun rises and man goes forth to his work. Death is a sleeping time for the body. Life is a working time. A Christian has no time to lie fallow. Philippians 2:12: "Work out your salvation with fear and trembling." John 9:4: "Work while it is day." Still there is some work to do, either some sin to mortify or some grace to exercise.

4. And last, if a day is once past, you can never call that day again. So once this day of life is past and gone, you cannot call it back.

USE 1. The thought that our life is but a day may serve to cool the intemperate heat of our affection for earthly things. We should not be greatly raised in the enjoyment of them, nor much dejected in the lack of them. These worldly comforts are not to be with us long, only a few days. Nay, it is but a day. Why, then, should we be too much taken up with them? Our life being so transient, made up of a few flying minutes, should much abate our affections for all things under the sun. I read that Abraham bought a burying place, Genesis 49:30. The longest possession we have here on earth is the possession of a burying place. So much for the first particular, a description of life; it is not measured by years but days. Nay, it is shorter; it is but a day.

The second thing in the text is the determination of a man's life in these words: "my appointed time," or "the days of my appointed time." The Hebrew has a double significance:
1. It signifies the length of our warfare: "the days of my warfare." Hence note this—the Christian's life here on earth is nothing other than warfare. 1 Timothy 1:18: "That thou mightest war a good warfare." It is not an easy life, a life of sloth and pleasure; it is warfare: "all the days of my warfare." A Christian's life is a warfare in three respects—in respect of hardship, watchfulness, and combat.
First, in respect of hardships. A soldier endures much hardship. He does not have his soft bed nor his dainty fare, but goes through many a tedious march. Such is a Christian's life. 2 Timothy 2:3: "Thou therefore endure hardship as a good soldier of Jesus Christ." We must not be, as Tertullian said, silken Christians,

but should expect to wrestle with difficulties. Second, a Christian's life is a warfare in respect of watchfulness. We must stand sentinel and be ever upon our guard. The soldier gets up into the watchtower and sends out his scouts lest the enemy should surprise him. It was Christ's watchword in Mark 13:37: "I say unto you all, Watch." A subtle heart needs a watchful eye. Watch lest sin decoys you, lest Satan falls upon you when you are asleep on your guard. When you have been praying against sin, then you must watch against temptation.

Third, a Christian's life is a warfare for combat. All of us come into the world as into a battlefield. We stand just as the Jews did in Nehemiah 4:17: "Everyone with one of his hands wrought in the work, and in the other hand held a weapon." Just such is our military posture, working and fighting in order to get this holy warfare. We must get our spiritual armor ready, the breastplate of holiness which can never be shot through; and having gotten this armor and the shield of faith in our hands, we must now do battle with our spiritual enemies. 2 Timothy 4:7: "I have fought the good fight of faith." Yea, and we must maintain a combat with the flesh, and that for an enemy, Satan.

To encourage us in this warfare, consider these two things:

We have a good captain, Jesus Christ. He is called the captain of our salvation, Hebrews 2:10. Christ not only leads us in our march and gives us skill to fight, but He gives us strength also. A captain may give his soldiers armor, but he cannot give them strength to fight—but Christ does. Isaiah 41:10: "I will strengthen thee, yea, I will help thee."

To encourage us in this warfare against sin and Satan, having overcome our ghostly enemy we shall have a glorious recompense of reward. "Henceforth is laid up for me a crown of righteousness," 2 Timothy 4:8. A crown is not fit for everyone; a crown is not fit for every head, but only for princes, kings, and persons of renown. After our combat with sin and Satan, God will call us out of the field where the bullets of temptation flew so fast and will give us a victorious crown. Then there will be no more battle, but there shall be music—not the drum and the cannon, but the violin and the harp, Revelation 14:2.

USE 2. Is life a warfare? How unworthy and blamable are they who have no spiritual artillery, nor make out against their spiritual enemies? They spend their time dressing themselves but do not put on their holy armor and rejoice in the sound of the organ. They spend their days in mirth, as if their lives were rather for music than for battle.

I have read of one who would have no man's name written upon his tomb but he who died manly in war. God writes no man's name in the Book of Life but such as die in this holy war, who die in battle fighting this good fight of faith.

2. Let us consider this word in the text in the other meaning: "the days of my apponted time." Hence observe:

DOCTRINE. God has preordained the just time and period of every man's life.

Job 14:5: "His days are determined; Thou hast appointed the bounds that he cannot pass." God, who numbers our hairs, numbers our days. He has entered down in His decree how long our lives shall last; and we shall not live one hour or minute beyond the time prefixed. Therefore, do not say, "If such a casualty had not happened; if such a friend had not died so soon."

OBJECTION. But is it not said in Ecclesiastes 7:17, "Be not over much wicked, why shouldest thou die before thy time?"

ANSWER. There is a general time of life and there is a limited time of life. There is a general time, with regard to the course of nature, and there is a limited time with regard to God's decree, how long such a person shall live. Now a man who dies young or dies a violent death dies before his time with regard to the course of nature; but he does not die before the time that God has limited and appointed.

USE 3. This should admonish us all to beware of adjourning and putting off our repentance. Our days are certain to God but they are uncertain to us. The Lord knows how long our glass will be running. For all we know there are but a few sands more to run. Life may expire in an instant. When our breath goes out we know not whether we shall draw it in again. It is true, Hezekiah had a lease sealed him of fifteen years, but we have no such lease. We are tenants at will and may be turned out presently. Our time of life is known to God but not to us. Take heed, therefore, of procrastinating and delaying. Death may be sent to any of you this night with a *habeas corpus*. God may say, "Give an account of your stewardship."

Is the time of our life appointed and the number of our days set? Why then, this should teach us courage for God. Be not fearful of doing your duty to appear for God, to own His cause in an idolatrous generation, to vindicate God's truth wherein His glory is con-

cerned. So the text says that our time is appointed.
Men can take away our liberty when they will, but they
shall not touch a hair of our heads till God's time is
come. This made our blessed Savior so zealous for His
Father's honor, so sharp in His reproof against sin.
Why was Christ so courageous? John 8:20, His hour was
not yet come. Christ knew full well that all His enemies
could not take away His life till the time was come
which His Father had appointed. This should make us
like Athanasius, that bulwark of the nation.

The third thing in the text is Job's holy resolution:
"I will wait till my change comes"; that is, I will wait till
death comes. Hence note:
DOCTRINE. Death, whenever it comes, makes a
great change.
First, this change that death will make is a certain
change; there is no avoiding it. Psalm 89:48: "What
man is he that lives and shall not see death?" See also
Hebrews 9:27. It is not strength, it is not courage, it is
not any worldly grandeur that can exempt from death.
Death's sword cuts asunder the royal scepter. The
godly must die as well as others. Though death does
not destroy the treasure of grace, yet death breaks the
vessel that this treasure is in. Pliny speaks of a golden
vine that is not subject to storms. The body of a saint,
when glorified, shall be like that golden vine; but now
it is a withering vine and is soon blasted by death. We
are not so sure to lie down in our beds as we are to lie
down in our graves.
Second, the change that death makes is a visible
change. How strangely is the body metamorphosed at
death. One scarcely knows their friends, they are so

disfigured by death! The eyes are hollow, the jaws are
fallen; death carries away all the goodly spoil of beauty.
It changes a living body into a carcass, Psalm 39:11:
"Thou makest his beauty to consume like a moth."
Take a body of the finest spinning, the lily and the
purple, white and ruddy. Once death like a moth gets
into it, it consumes all the luster and glory of it. Death
puts the body into a very frightful dress that nothing
can fall in love with but worms.

Third, the change that death makes is often a very
sudden change. Death steals upon some unawares. I
have read of one who was suddenly choked with the
kernel of a grape. What quick dispatch do several dis-
tempers make! Death oftentimes strikes and gives no
warning.

Fourth, and last, the change that death makes is an
unalterable change. As the tree falls, so it lies to eternity. Death is a change that puts us into an unchangeable condition.

Application

First, see what a different change death makes to
the righteous and to the wicked. Both are changed at
death, but there is a vast difference.

1. Death makes a dreadful change to the wicked; it
is a trap door to let them down to hell. There are some
wicked who live here in gallantry and splendor, who
are clothed in purple and fare deliciously every day;
oh, but when death comes they will find an alteration!
Death will throw the wicked down from the top of the
pinnacle of their honor. I allude to Revelation 18:22,

"The voice of the harper shall be heard no more in thee."

There is a river in America that runs in the day, but at night it is dried up. So these pleasures that now run in the lifetime in a flowing stream shall all, at the night of death, be dried up. Nor will the ungodly only lose their sugared things. But here is their misery—their souls must be steeped in the flames of hell, Mark 9:44, where the worm dies not. Such a fire is kindled in God's anger that no tears can quench it, nor can any time finish it.

We read of the servant under the Law that, if he had a hard master, yet at the end of seven years there was a jubilee, a year of release when the servant might go from him. But in hell's torments there is no year of jubilee, Revelation 9:6. Men shall seek death and shall not find it. If a spark of God's anger falling into a man's conscience is so full of torture in this life, oh, then, how terrible will it be to have the fire of God's wrath to lie in forever! Thus you see death will be a sad change to the unrighteous. Therefore, surely the very thoughts of death must be terrible to a wicked man.

2. It will be a glorious change to all the righteous persons. They shall have their fetters of sin knocked off and shall drink of the rivers of pleasure. Oh, blessed change! From a weary pilgrimage to a blessed paradise; from labor to eternal rest. In short, death to a child of God is a friend. Death is a pale horse to carry a believer home to his Father's house. Death gives a full possession of glory. There is a freehold in law and there is a freehold in deed. A believer now has a freehold in law, that is, he has a right to heaven; but at death he has a freehold in deed. He makes entry of it and takes pos-

session.

Death pulls down this old building, this house of clay, and prepares for the soul a better house, a house not made with hands. Oh, blessed change to the righteous! And this may be a comfort in the death of Christian friends. Whenever they are changed by death they are sure to change for the better; they go instantly into a blessed eternity.

USE OF EXHORTATION.

Does death make such a change, a certain change, a visible change and, sometimes, an unalterable change? Let us all labor to be fitted for this great change. It is a very sad thing, as Job said, to have the grave ready for us and us not ready for the grave. When death surprises the unprepared soul, what a condition will he be in! He will say as those, "Oh, death! I pray thee, let me be excused one day more, one hour more, to prepare myself." But death will neither be bribed nor courted.

Job cursed the day of his birth; unprepared souls will curse the day of their death. Oh, then, be fitted for this last end! And for the purpose labor for a holy change. Get grace into your souls. Death cannot hurt grace. Grace is armor-proof; it can never be shot through. Grace is as needful for the soul as oil is for the lamp. Christians, get holy hearts. Be as Christ's bride: get yourselves ready. Dress yourselves every day by the glass of God's Word. See your spots in a glass, and, when you have seen them, wash them off by repenting tears. Adorn the hidden man of your hearts with love, meekness, and holiness, and put on the Lord Jesus, which is your clothing of wrought gold. By having this holy change wrought, you will be fitted for your last and great change.

To conclude all, you who are prepared, live in a continual expectation of this great change. So did Job in the text: "I will wait till my change comes." First, live in hope till this change comes. Second, be patient till this change comes.

First, live in hope till this change comes. The word in the text is "I will wait." In the Hebrew it is "I will hope till my change comes." The husbandman, having sown his seed, hopes for a crop. Having sown the seed of true repentance, he now hopes for a full crop of glory at death.

Second, and last, be patient till this change comes. "I will wait," said Job. In the Greek it is "I will be patient till my change comes."

Indeed, the troubles that the righteous suffer here, and that great preferment they shall have in heaven, may be ready to cause impatience to stay here any longer. But take heed of this. We must not be our own carvers. God knows the best season when He will send for His children home. Therefore we must wait but a while. Then we shall enjoy our wish, and that is to have Christ's sweet embraces, and to lie in the bosom of divine love.

His Heart Is Fixed

"He shall not be afraid of evil tidings; his heart is fixed, trusting in the Lord." Psalm 112:7

"A word fitly spoken," said Solomon, "is like apples of gold in pictures of silver." In this respect I have chosen this Scripture to treat at this time. When the winds begin to rise and a storm threatens, it is time to get our spiritual tackling ready and to cast anchor. The mariner casts his anchor downward; the Christian casts his anchor upward within the veil. In the deepest danger, he casts out the sweet anchor of faith and is not afraid. So says the text, "He shall not be afraid of evil tidings; his heart is fixed, trusting in the Lord."

In this Psalm you have described the character of a righteous man, verse 1—he delights greatly in God's commands. He not only keeps God's commands, but he loves them. They are the joy of his heart. He delights greatly in God's commands.

In this Psalm is set down the righteous man's happiness several ways:

First, his children shall be blessed. Verse 2: "His seed shall be mighty upon earth." Righteousness entails mercy upon posterity.

Second, his estate shall be blessed. Verse 3: "Wealth and riches shall be in his house." A man is no loser by being righteous; it makes his estate flourish.

Third, his soul shall be blessed, verse 9. It is righteousness that shall endure forever; that is, the joy and comfort of it endures forever. His grace shall be crowned with glory. This flower of paradise does not wither.

Fourth, the righteous man's name shall be blessed. Verse 6: "The righteous shall be had in everlasting remembrance." That is, his name shall be honored; it shall live when he is dead. The righteous man carries a good conscience with him when he dies and leaves a good name behind him. He shall be in everlasting remembrance. And so I come to the text. This righteous man shall not be afraid of evil tidings, for "his heart is fixed, trusting in the Lord."

The text consists of these two general parts:

First, the righteous man's privilege: "He shall not be afraid of evil tidings."

Second, the ground or reason for it: "His heart is fixed, trusting in the Lord."

I begin with the first of these briefly, the righteous man's privilege: "He shall not be afraid of evil tidings." When there are rumors of evil approaching, the godly man shall not be discomposed in his mind. He shall not be in a panic or fear. Yet let me insert this for the right understanding of it.

First, not that the righteous man is insensible of danger, or how else could he humble himself under God's mighty hand?

Second, not but that some clouds of fear may arise in his mind. Though grace subdues, it does not expel nature. But the meaning of the text is this: "He shall not be afraid of evil tidings." That is, a righteous man shall not be afraid with a distracting fear. Such a fear takes him off from duty and quite untunes him for God's service.

"He shall not be afraid of evil tidings" with a fainting fear so as to have his heart die within him. Thus it was with Saul, 1 Samuel 28:20. Saul fell straightaway all along upon the earth and was sore afraid. He fainted away in his fear.

A righteous man shall not be afraid of evil tidings with a despairing fear. He shall not so fear but that the heart still sweetly rests upon God's promises. It is with a godly man in time of danger as it is with a ship that lies at anchor. A ship at anchor shakes a little on the water, but it is fixed, being at anchor. So, though there may be some shakings and tremblings in the flesh, yet a Christian is not so tossed with fear, but he is like a ship at anchor. "His heart is fixed, trusting in the Lord."

USE. See the difference between the godly and the wicked. The godly man is not afraid of evil rumors. He does not fear with a distracting or desponding fear; hope is still preserved and kept alive in the soul. But when the wicked see danger approaching, they are surprised with heart-killing fears. Isaiah 33:14: "The sinners in Zion are afraid: fearfulness hath surprised hypocrites." Guilt is the bladder of fear. When Adam had stolen the fruit, then he began to tremble. "I was afraid," he said to God, "and hid myself." Sinners fall into convulsions of conscience. Cain's mark was a shaking in the flesh. And a wicked man has a trembling in his heart. Isaiah 13:8: "They shall be afraid." The Hebrew word for fear signifies such a fright as casts women into travail and makes them miscarry. So sinners shall be cast, as it were, into such a fright as their faces shall be ashamed. What is that? That is, when troubles arise their faces wax pale. So much for the first thing in the text, the righteous man's privilege: "He shall not be afraid of evil tidings" with a distracting or desponding fear.

Second, here in these words is the ground or reason why a godly person shall not be afraid or amazed at evil tidings: "His heart is fixed, trusting in the Lord." There is the ground. This makes him as the leviathan, without fear: "His heart is fixed, trusting in the Lord."

So the observation is this:

DOCTRINE. It is the genius and temperament of a true saint, in times of imminent danger, to have his heart fixed by trusting in the Lord Jehovah.

His heart is fixed, trusting in the Lord. For the illustration of this proposition I shall answer these three questions:

1. What is it to trust in God in times of danger?
2. Why ought we to trust in God?
3. How does trusting in God fix the heart?

I begin with the first of these.

QUESTION 1. What is it to trust in God in times of danger?

ANSWER. It is called in Scripture a "casting our burden upon God," the burden of our care, the burden of our fear, the burden of our wants, the burden of our sins. Psalm 55:22: "Cast thy burden upon the Lord, and He shall sustain thee."

Trusting in God in Scripture is called a staying ourselves upon God, as a man who is ready to fall stays himself upon some prop or pillow. Thus a Christian stays himself upon God, Isaiah 5:10. I shall describe trusting in God thus: It is a heroic act of faith whereby we roll all our care and lay the stress of our salvation only upon God.

Now there is required in this trusting in God an absolutely necessary knowledge and an absolutely necessary acquaintance with Him.

First, knowledge of God. Psalm 9:10: "They that know Thy name will put their trust in Thee."

Second, in this trusting in God is required acquaintance with Him through Christ. Without acquaintance there can be no trust; one cannot well trust a stranger. There must be some acquaintance with God. Job 22:21: "Acquaint thyself now with Him and be at peace." That's the first point, what this trusting in God is.

QUESTION 2. Why ought we to trust in God?
I will give you but these two reasons.

ANSWER 1. Because God calls for this trust. Isaiah 26:4: "Trust ye in the Lord forever." Psalm 62:8: "Trust in Him at all times." Though you are in never such straits and fears, yet remember to cast anchor upwards. Trust in God at all times. The Lord would take off our confidence and trusting in other things besides Him. Jeremiah 17:5: "Cursed be the man that trusteth in man, and maketh flesh his arm." We break our crutches because we lean too hard on them. God would have us make Him our trust. And the truth is, trust and affiance is the chief part of the worship we ascribe to God.

ANSWER 2. We must trust in God in all our straits and dangers. He is the proper object of our trust. My brethren, the creature is not a fit object of our trust as appears thus—it has two ill qualities that we cannot

repose our trust in: the creature deceives and it fails. I
shall deal only with the first.

The creature deceives. It is but a sugared lie. Where
we think to suck honey, we taste only wormwood. And
as it deceives, so it fades and withers. Like a rose, the
fuller it is blown the sooner it sheds. So we cannot
make the creature the object of our trust, but God deserves our trust. He is called in Scripture a strong tower
where you may have safety. Proverbs 18:10: "The name
of the Lord is a strong tower." He is El-Shaddai, God
Almighty, Genesis 17:1. There is no condition we can
be in, no exigency, but He can relieve. He is God
Almighty.

In particular, there are two glorious attributes in
God in which we may safely repose our trust. The one
is His mercy, the other is His truth. They are both
joined in one verse: "Thou wilt perform Thy truth to
Jacob and Thy mercy to Abraham," Micah 7:20.

First, we may rest and stay our souls upon God's
mercy. Psalm 13:5: "I have trusted in Thy mercy."
Though I have sinned, mercy can pardon me. Though
I am in want, mercy can relieve me. God's mercy is infinite; it is a honeycomb for sweetness and a rock for
safety.

Second, we may safely rely on God's truth or faith-
fulness. Remember this—truth is the object of trust.
Heaven and earth may sooner fail than God's veracity.
Psalm 89:33: "I will not suffer My faithfulness to fail."
Good reason, then, why we should trust in God. Where
can we pitch our faith but upon God's faithfulness?

QUESTION 3. How does trusting in God fix the
heart? That is the third thing I wish to show you, that

trusting in God is the way to have the heart fixed. "His heart is fixed, trusting in the Lord." ANSWER. Note two things. First, it is an excellent thing to have the heart fixed. Second, it is only faith that fixes the heart.

First, it is a rare thing. It is excellent to have the heart fixed. This appears two ways: 1. Fixing the heart shows solid efficacy of spirit. A heart unfixed is just like a ship without ballast, blown up and down in the water. 2. Fixing the heart is for holy duties. He whose heart is fixed upon God serves God with delight, with cheerfulness. Indeed, a heart unfixed is a heart unfit for duty. A shaking hand is not fit to write. An unfixed heart is unfit to pray or meditate; it runs after other vanities. Surely, then, a fixed frame of heart is an excellent frame of heart. You know that when the milk is settled it turns to cream. So, when the heart is settled and fixed on God, it is ever in the best frame. That's the first thing.

Second, trusting in God fixes the heart. The heart is fixed, trusting in the Lord; that is, it is fixed by trusting. Faith frees the heart from those commotions which cause trembling and quivering. It fixes the heart upon God. As a star is fixed in its orb, so a believer's soul is fixed on God. Faith makes the heart cleave to God as a needle cleaves to the magnet. Faith fixes the heart. Such a fixed star was Athanasius. Tertullian called him an invincible adamant. He could not be stirred away from the truth. Faith had fixed his heart on God. Now I will make some use of this point.

USE OF INFORMATION. Here you see the misery of wicked men. They are unfixed; they do not know where to rest when troubles come; they have no God to trust. Sinners are like a ship without anchor, tossed with the storms, that has nowhere to put in for harbor. They are like the old world—when the flood came they had no ark to trust. The wicked are like King Saul in an hour of danger. 1 Samuel 28:15: "I am sorely distressed; for the Philistines make war against me, and God is departed from me." A flagitious sinner is like a soldier in battle where the bullets are flying about and he is without armor and has no garrison to trust. Beloved, it is faith that makes the heart fixed in troublesome times. Faith engarrisons the soul in God's attributes and makes it like a tower walled in with rocks that is impregnable.

USE OF EXHORTATION. Oh! Let us above all things labor for this heart-fixing grace of faith. Trusting in God corroborates and animates and bears the heart up in death-threatening dangers. Oh, get this heart-fixing grace of faith!

But alas! Who will *not* say that he is resolved and fixed? If a storm arises, he, for his part, trusts in God. Who will *not* say he trusts in God?

Therefore, we must bring our heart to a Scriptural touchstone. It is worthwhile. Let us try whether our trusting in God is right or not. You shall know it thus:

First, if our trust is right, then we commit our chief treasure to God. Our soul is the jewel, the chief treasure, and we commit this to God's care and custody. Psalm 31:5: "Into thy hand I commit my spirit." We lay up all our hope in God. Psalm 39:7: "What wait I for?

Lord, my hope is in Thee." As in time of war a man puts all his money and plate in a safe, strong place, so must we lay up all our hopes in God as a strong tower.

Second, if we trust in God aright, why then, in all our danger we fly to God. There are some who, when trouble arises, fly to their shifts. Oh! But do we fly to God? Psalm 143:9: "Deliver me, O Lord, from mine enemies. I will fly to Thee to hide me." When Satan shoots his fiery darts of temptation, then we fly under Christ's wing to shelter us. When a hawk pursues the dove, it casts itself into the clefts of the rock, and there it hides. So, when Satan pursues us with temptation, we get into the bleeding wounds of Christ, these clefts of the Rock, and there we rest and are safe. Augustine said, "I lay myself softly, and rest upon my Savior's bleeding wounds."

Third, if we trust in God aright, then we can repose our trust in God when all creature refuges fail us, Habakkuk 1:7. Though the fig tree should not blossom, can we rely upon God, upon His promises, upon His attributes? Can we trust in God in the deficiency of second causes? Can we trust God without a pawn? Can we go to heaven without crutches? Then our trust is genuine, a true trust. When the pipes are cut that used to bring us comfort, can we still say, "Yet all our fresh springs are in God"? Psalm 87:7.

Fourth, we may know if our trust in God is right by having a spirit of courage infused into us. Unbelief breeds fear; faith breeds courage, Proverbs 28:1. The righteous man is bold as a lion. Faith enables a man to appear in a good cause and to withstand all opposition. Daniel 3:18: "Be it known to thee, O king, we will not serve thy gods, nor worship thy golden images." See

Hebrews 10:34. Such an invincible Christian was Basil the Great, who did not fear the threats of the emperor. He was like a rock which no water could shake.

Fifth, we may know our trust is right when we obey God in all things He calls for. There are two things in holy trust: there is affiance and obedience, Romans 16:26. Observe, they who expect what God promises will perform what God commands, Psalm 26:1. They have trusted in the Lord. Where was the trial of this trust? Psalm 119:66: "I have kept Thy commandments." They deceive themselves who say that they trust in God and yet will not serve Him. They deny to give God the kiss of obedience.

Sixth, true trusting in God is purifying. "Having purified their hearts by faith." Faith purges out the love of sin as medicine purges out noxious temperaments. 1 Timothy 3:9: "Holding the mystery of faith in a pure conscience." Faith is the wedding grace that marries Christ, and holiness is the child that faith brings forth. The woman in the gospel who touched Christ by faith felt a healing virtue coming from Him. Let not that man say his heart is fixed, trusting in God, who allows himself in any sin. What, trust in God and yet swear and be drunk and unclean! This is not trust; it is presumption! Just like those Jews in Jeremiah 3:4-5, "Wilt thou not cry unto Me, My Father?" What follows? "Behold, thou hast done evil things as thou couldst." Those hypocrites would call God Father, yet they sinned as fast as they could.

Seventh, true trusting in God is a patient waiting, a waiting trust. Psalm 37:7: "Rest in the Lord and wait patiently for Him." Though a believer does not have what he desires immediately upon the return of a prayer, those smiles and love tokens from God as he desires, yet he is resolved that he will be in a waiting posture. He will wait till mercy comes. That's a fine Scripture, Psalm 123:2: "Our eyes wait upon the Lord our God, until He have mercy upon us." That man who has no patience to wait has not faith to trust. Remember Isaiah 28:16: "He that believeth maketh not haste." A believer knows full well that the longer he stays for a mercy the richer it will be when it comes. The longest voyages have the greatest returns. Thus you see what this trusting in God is that fixes the heart in evil times.

Now let me, in a few words, resume the exhortation. Oh! Let us labor for this true faith and trust, to have our hearts fixed on God in evil times. When all is done, faith is the heart-establishing grace. Psalm 112:8: "His heart is established." The Hebrew word for establish signifies this: "the heart is shored up." It is a metaphor that alludes to a house that is shored up by pieces of timber. Thus faith shores up the heart when it is likely to sink. Oh! Get this heart-fixing grace of faith. Thus you come to be resolved and undaunted even in the worst of times and dangers.

Now, that we may labor thus, consider but these three things:

First, there is nothing but God we can fix our trust in. Alas! Whatever else we trust besides God will prove an ark of bulrushes; it will never shelter us in an hour of danger. There is no trusting in riches. Proverbs 23:5: "Riches take themselves wings and fly."

There is no trusting in friends; they may die, or, which is worse, they may deceive, Micah 7:5. Our Lord

Jesus was betrayed by a friend.

There is no trusting in great men; who can trust those who are not true to God? Psalm 118:9: "It is better to trust in the Lord than to put confidence in princes."

There is no trusting in your own hearts. Why, alas! The heart is full of lust, full of deceit. It is a bosom traitor. Proverbs 28:26: "He that trusts in his own heart is a fool." Oh! But my brethren, trust in God; He is a never-failing refuge. A little boat, while it is tied fast to a rock, is very safe. So, when the soul is tied by faith to Christ Jesus, the Rock of Ages, then it is safe. Psalm 46:11: "My God is the Rock of my refuge."

Second, fixing our trust in God brings sweet peace with it. Peace is the olive branch that faith brings in its mouth. Turn to that excellent Scripture, Isaiah 26:3: "Thou wilt keep him in perfect peace, whose mind is stayed on Thee, because he trusts in Thee." Pray, observe: perfect trust is blessed with perfect peace. The word "trust in God" comes from the Hebrew word which signifies to nourish. Why so? Because our trusting in God nourishes, it cherishes peace in the soul. Faith represents God as reconciled, and this gives peace. He who trusts in God has peace in the midst of storms and tempests. He is like Noah in the ark; when the deluge came he could sit and sing in the ark.

Third, and last, fixing our trust on God is that which brings in mercy, comfort, and deliverance to us. Psalm 32:2: "He that trusts in God, mercy shall compass him about." Would it not be a fine thing, in the midst of a fight, to be compassed about with a golden shield that no arrow or bullet could pierce? It is true, God's mercy, like a golden shield, shall compass him about. Oh, therefore, get this heart-fixing grace of faith!

To encourage your faith, remember these two things, you who travail for the church's deliverance: faith and prayer are the two midwives that deliver God's Church when she is in travail. I will give you a clear Scripture, 2 Chronicles 4:11, "Help us, O Lord"— there was prayer; "for we rest on Thee"—there was faith. When we build our affiance and confidence on God, He is obliged in point of honor to defend and save us. Isaiah 28:7: "My heart trusted in Thee, and I am helped."

To shut up all, let us above all things labor to have our hearts fixed on God by holy trust. Trust Him where you cannot trace Him. Trust God for protection in this life, and salvation in the other life.

My beloved, trusting in God is a prescription for all diseases. Faith is the cure. Does the orphan trust himself and his estate in the hands of his guardian? Does the patient trust his life in the hands of the physician? And shall we not trust our souls in God's hand? 2 Samuel 22:31: "He is a buckler to all them that trust in Him." If ever we would get mastery of our fears and disquiets, let us captivate carnal reason and advance faith. So, then, you shall not be afraid of evil tidings, for the heart will be fixed, trusting in the Lord.

Light in Darkness

"Unto the upright there ariseth light in darkness." Psalm 112:4

Chrysostom calls the Scriptures a spiritual paradise. The Book of Psalms is placed in the midst of this paradise. David's Psalms are not only for delight but for benefit. They are like those trees of the sanctuary in Ezekiel, which were both for food and for medicine. The Psalms are commensurate and exactly fitted to every Christian's condition. If his affections are frozen, here he may fetch fire; if he is weak in grace, here he may fetch armor; if he is ready to fain, here he may fetch cordials.

Among other divine consolations, this text is none of the least: "Unto the upright there ariseth light in darkness." These words are calculated for the comfort of God's Church in all ages. This text is like Israel's pillar of fire, which gave light in the wilderness. Or it is like the mariner's lantern, to give light in a dark night.

"To the upright there ariseth light in darkness." Give me leave to explain the words, then I shall come to the proposition.

"To the upright." Who are meant here by the upright? The Hebrew word for upright signifies plainness of heart. The upright man is without blushing or fraud. He is one in whose spirit there is no guile, Psalm 32:2. He who is upright, his heart and his tongue go together, as a well-made dial goes exactly by the sun. The words following here in the text may serve for a short paraphrase to show us who this upright man is. He is gracious, full of compassion, and righteous.

1. He is gracious—that implies his holiness.
2. He is full of compassion—that implies his charitableness.
3. He is righteous—that implies his justness.

The upright man is gracious; therefore he fears God. He is full of compassion; therefore he feeds the poor. He is righteous; therefore he does to others as he would have them to him. The upright man is one who acts from a right principle, and that is faith. By a right rule, and that's the Word of God; to a right end, and that's the glory of God: this is the downright upright man.

The second thing in the text is: "There ariseth light to the upright man." By light is here meant, metaphorically, comfort or joy, Esther 8:16. The Jews had light, gladness, and joy; but by light is meant gladness. The light, when it springs, very much relieves. Joy is to the heart as light is to the eye—very exhilarating and refreshing.

Third, "light ariseth in darkness." By darkness is meant trouble, anything that disquiets either the body or the mind. Trouble is darkness. Isaiah 8:22: "Look unto the earth and behold trouble and darkness." Psalm 107:10: "Such as sit in darkness, and in the shadow of death." As darkness is very disconsolate and frightening, so where trouble comes it makes everything look like the terrors of the night.

The observation is this:

DOCTRINE. When the condition of God's people is darkness, God causes a light to shine unto them. "To the upright there ariseth light in darkness."

Here are two branches of the proposition. First, the upright, such whom God loves, have their night. Second, a morning light arises to them in the midst of all their darkness.

First, the upright have their night; it may be a very dark season. Godliness does not exempt them from suffering. They may have a night of affliction; a cloud may set upon their names and estates. God may lay an embargo upon all their outward comforts, Ruth 1:20.

Moreover, the people of God may have a night of desertion. God may withdraw the smiling beams of His favor, and then it is night with them indeed. Job 6:4: "The arrows of the Almighty are within me; the poison thereof drinks up my spirits." It alludes, said Grotius, to the Persians who, in their war, dip their arrows in poison to make their wounds more deadly. Thus God sometimes shoots the poisonous arrows of desertion at the godly. Then they are in the dark. They are benighted. Though God has the heart of a Father, yet sometimes He has the look of an enemy. He may cause darkness in the soul and shut up the beams of spiritual comfort.

He does this that He may the more quicken the exercise of grace, for prayer may sometimes act highest in the hour of desertion. Jonah 2:4: "I said I was cast out of Thy sight; yet will I look towards Thy holy temple." Faith and patience, like two stars, shine most bright in the night of desertion. We are taken with the comfort, but God is more taken with the actings of our graces.

The Lord may cause a dark cloud to be upon the righteous, a cloud of desertion, that He may hereby awaken and stir up in His people a spirit of prayer that they may now cry mightily to God, that they may stir up themselves to take hold of God by prayer. Sometimes a father hides his face to make the child cry after him more. So God may hide His face in a cloud of desertion that His children may cry the more after Him. Psalm 140:7: "Oh, hide not Thy face from me!" Desertion will make one pray if anything will. Desertion is a short hell. Jonah called the whale's belly the belly of hell because he was deserted there. And if ever he was going to pray it was now, that he might get out of that hell. Jonah 2:2: "Out of the belly of hell I cried unto Thee, and Thou heardest my voice."

That's the first point, the godly may have their night.

The second part of the proposition is this: A morning light arises in the righteous in all their darkness.

"To the upright there ariseth light in the darkness." Psalm 18:28: "The Lord will light my candle." As if David had said, "My comforts at present seem to be blown out, and I am in the dark. But the Lord will light my candle and cause light to arise."

There is a twofold light that God causes to arise in His people in the dark—an outward light and an inward light.

An outward light shines; that is, God oftentimes causes the light of prosperity to arise upon His people, that is, a light in darkness. When God causes peace and prosperity in the tabernacle of the righteous, here is light rising in darkness. Job 29:3: "When His candle shineth upon my head." The candle is the candle of prosperity, a lamp of outward blessings. God has suddenly altered the scene of providence; all of a sudden He has turned the shadows of death into the light of morning.

When God's people are in the dark, God sometimes causes an inward light to arise in them.

First, the light of grace; He makes that shine. In the midst of darkness, a spark of faith in the soul is a spark of light. When the tree has no blossoms or leaves to be seen, as in autumn, there may yet be sap in the root of the vine.

So, my brethren, when our outward comforts are dead, as it were, it is autumn; yet there may be the seed of God in the heart. And this spark of grace is a dawning light to the soul.

Second, God sometimes causes a light of spiritual joy and consolation to arise in the dark and disconsolate soul. And truly this light of spiritual joy is the very glimmering of the light of heaven. Isaiah 12:1: "Thine anger is turned away, and Thou comfortest me." This light of spiritual comfort is sweet and ravishing. It as far exceeds all other joys as heaven excels earth. Thus you see in the midst of darkness or black clouds that God makes light to arise and shine unto the godly. It is only God Himself who can make it lightsome when the soul is in a dark, disconsolate condition. When the sun sets, none can make it rise but God. So, when it is sunset in the soul and the dew of tears drops, none can make daylight in that soul but God Himself. Others may preach comfort to us, but it is God who must make us feel comfort. Others may bring a cordial to us, and set it to us and by us, but it is God who must pour in this cordial. Psalm 4:7: "Thou, Lord, hast put gladness in my heart."

QUESTION. Why does God make light and joy to arise to the upright in their darkness?
ANSWER. For three reasons:
1. That He may fulfill His promises. He has said that He will give light to His people when they are in darkness. Isaiah 42:16: "I will make darkness light before them." God's honor lies upon it to make good His promise. He causes light to spring up in the disconsolate soul. God's promise is His bond. When a man has given his bond, he cannot well go back. God's promises may be long in travail, yet at last they bring forth. There are two things in God that never fail.

First, His compassions fail not, Lamentations 3:22.

Second, His faithfulness fails not, Psalm 89:33. God may sometimes delay a promise, but He will never deny His promise. God may sometimes change His promise, or He may turn a temporal promise into a spiritual promise, but He will never break His promise. He has said He will cause light to go before His people in all their darkness.

2. God will cause light to arise in His people in all their darkness because they help to enlighten others, and therefore they shall not lack light. When others are in the dark of ignorance, they enlighten them with knowledge. When others are in the dark of affliction, they relieve them. They are merciful to them in giving them alms, which administer light and joy to their hearts. The saints of God are lights to those who sit in darkness. When they are benighted with any sorrow, they shall not lack comfort. The Lord causes light to

arise to them in darkness.

3. God will cause light to arise in His people in darkness; either He will support them in trouble or deliver them out of trouble. He will cause light to arise because He sees His people have need, great need of some dawnings of light. They would faint away and be discouraged if there was nothing but darkness and no glimmering of light.

Should the sick patient always have purging medicine and no cordials given him, he would faint away. God knows our frame, and He sees our spirits would fail before Him if He always suffered a cloud to lie upon us. Therefore, in judgment He remembers mercy. He causes the daystar of comfort to arise upon His people. God will not let it be always be midnight lest we touch upon the rock of despair. The musician will not stretch the strings of his violin too far lest they break asunder. Thus you see why the wise God sees it best to cause light to arise in the midst of darkness.

So much for the doctrinal part.

USE 1. OF INFERENCE.

INFERENCE 1. See the infinite goodness of God towards His people in all cases that fall out in this world, whether affliction or desertion. Oh, the goodness of God! The Lord checkers His work; He mixes some stars to give light as the artist mixes bright colors with dark shadows. The condition of God's people on earth is never so dark but they may see a rainbow in the cloud of providence. Take one Scripture to verify this. Psalm 138:7: "Though I walk in the midst of trouble, Thou wilt revive me." Every step I take I tread upon thorns; I walk in the midst of trouble.

Joseph was in prison, and there was darkness; but the text says, "The Lord was with Joseph," Genesis 39:21. There light arose. Jacob had the hollow of his thigh put out of joint—there was darkness; but at that very time he saw God's face, a dark glimmering of God, and the Lord blessed him—there was light rising in darkness, Genesis 32:25.

Job lost all he ever had and was struck with boils and sores; here was a dark providence. Yes, but hereby Job's grace was perfected and improved, and God gave him an honorable testimony that he was upright, and gave him double estate to what he had before—here was light arisen to Job in the clouds of darkness, Job 42:10.

Thus God mixes light with His people's darkness. In the ark there was manna laid up with the rod. So it is in God's providence towards His people. With the rod of affliction there is some manna, some light, some comfort that God causes to spring up. Manna with the rod, oh, the goodness of God! In the darkest night He keeps alive some spark of light among His people. That's the first inference.

INFERENCE 2. If it is God's work to cause light and comfort to the righteous, why then, how contrary do they act who make it their work to cause darkness and sorrow to the righteous! God's work is to cause light to spring up in the godly. Their work is to cause darkness. You know there is a woe that belongs to them who make the heart of the righteous sad. God is creating light for His people, and His enemies are laying snares for them. God is pouring wine and oil into His people's wounds, and His adversaries are pouring vinegar into those wounds.

How contrary do these act! Those who are of the
Romish whore are this day plotting the ruin of God's
people, and would have the Church of God lie in a
field of blood. The Lord makes light to arise to the
godly. The wicked labor to make darkness and sorrow
to arise for them. But such as lay snares for the righteous will find God raining fire upon them, Psalm 11:6.
Upon the wicked God shall rain fire and brimstone.
The wicked strike at Christ through His members'
sides; but let them know that if they kick against Christ
the Rock, the Lord will be too hard for them at last.
God ordains His arrows against the persecutors, Psalm
7:13, and God never misses His mark. If He has His arrow upon the string, He will certainly shoot; and He
never misses His mark. That's a second inference.

INFERENCE 3. See here the difference between
the wicked and the godly. In all their darkness, the
godly have some light; some comfort arises to them. In
all their comforts, the wicked have some darkness rising up to them. Conscience chides them and troubles
threaten them. It is like the handwriting upon the wall,
Psalm 68:31. God shall wound the heads of His enemies, and the hairy scalp of such a one as goes on still
in his trespasses. The sinner, in his light-hearted condition, in all his outward mirth, may see some clouds of
darkness. God's threatening arrows are against him
and God's curse is against him; and God's curse blasts
wherever it comes. An impenitent sinner lives every day
under the sentence of death, and there remains for
him, said the Apostle, a fiery indignation, Hebrews
10:27.

When the hardened sinner dies he will be in a bad
case; he drops into the grave and hell both at once.

God has brewed a deadly cup for the impenitent sinner. Observe Psalm 75:8: "In the hand of the Lord there is a cup, the wine is red, it is full of mixture, and the dregs thereof, the wicked of the earth shall wring them out, and drink them." This red wine is the wrath of God, and this wine is full of mixture. What's that? That's the worm of conscience and the fire of hell. Here is a mixed cup, and the wicked shall ever be drinking this cup. God will never say, "Let this cup pass away." No, they must be forever drinking the dregs of the cup of wrath. I think this Scripture should be a damp to all their joy and mirth. Darkness is coming upon them, 1 Samuel 28:19. It was sad news to Saul that the devil brought, "Tomorrow thou shalt be with me." Dreadful news! Now men are sporting with their lusts and pleasures; now they think they are in their gallantry, and tomorrow they may be with the devil.

INFERENCE 4. Does God cause light to spring up in His people's darkness? Then see here the difference between earth and heaven. Here in this world there is a mixture of darkness with the saints' light; in heaven there shall be nothing but pure light, no darkness there. It is called an inheritance of light, Colossians 1:12. As the philosophers say, light is the very glory of the creation. It is the beauty of the world. What was all the world without light but a dark prison? Here's the beauty of heaven, it is a place of light. There is no eclipse or dark shadow to be seen there. Heaven is a bright body all over embroidered with light. There is the Sun of righteousness shining with the bright orient beams of glory, Revelation 21:23. The Lamb is the light thereof. Oh, how should we long for that place of paradise!

USE 2. OF CONSOLATION.

This consolation is for the Church and people of God.

This text is a pillar of light, a breast of consolation. "To the upright ariseth light in darkness." Does God make light, joy, and peace to arise to the righteous? Why, then, should we despair? Why should we despond when it is God's great design to lighten His people's darkness? I confess things have a bad aspect. England is like the ship in the gospel, almost covered with waves. This may humble us and set our eyes abroach with tears, yet let us not mourn as without hope.

First, this text, I think, lets in some branches of light. It gives some spark of comfort in our darkness. Let me come as the dove with an olive branch of peace. That is some spark of light that there are many upright ones in the land. And the text says, "Light ariseth to the upright." Indeed, were the godly quite removed, as it is the desire of some to destroy them, God would soon make quick work with the nation. He would soon break up house here. Genesis 19:22: "Haste thee, escape thither: for I cannot do anything till thou be come thither." God will do much for the sake of the upright of whom my text speaks. The upright are the excellent of the earth; they are the chariots and horsemen of Israel. They are the very flower and cream of the creation; they are the glory of Christ, 2 Corinthians 8:23. And for their sakes God may yet cause light to arise, and His arm may bring salvation.

Second, another spark of light in our darkness that God is pleased to stir up in His people is a spirit of mighty prayer. They cry mightily. Certainly God will not say to this city and nation, "Seek ye My face in vain." Prayer is the wall and bulwark of the land. It is observable that when the Lord intends to pour out the vials of His indignation, He stops the sluices of prayer; He shuts up the spirit of prayer. Jeremiah 7:16: "Therefore, pray not thou for this people, neither lift up a cry nor prayer for them, neither make intercession to Me, for I will not hear." God has not yet said this to us.

The key of prayer, oiled with tears and turned with the hand of faith, unlocks God's bowels. Prayer, when it is importunate, staves off wrath from the nation, Exodus 32:10. God said to Moses, "Now therefore let Me alone, that My wrath may wax hot against them, and that I may consume them." And what did Moses do? He only prayed. Fervent prayer overcomes the Almighty. Prayer finds God free, but it leaves Him bound. It is as it was. His hand staves off judgment. This lets in some dawning to this land, that God doesn't wholly leave us, especially remembering that Christ Jesus, praying over our prayers again, presents them to His Father and perfumes them with His sweet odor which makes them go up as incense, Revelation 8:3.

Third, another spark arising is when we consider God's compassion and bowels of mercy. Mercy is God's darling attribute that He loves most of all to magnify, Micah 7:18. Mercy pleases Him. Justice is God's strange work, as if He was not used to it; but mercy is His proper work. It is as natural for Him to show mercy as for the bee to give honey. Why may not mercy give the casting voice for this nation? As that Scripture says, "In His love and in His pity He redeemed them," Isaiah 63:9. Love and pity will do great things.

God's mercy is not only free, sending out pardons where He pleases, but, which is more, God's mercy can as well heal as it can save. It is a healing mercy. Hosea 14:4: "I will heal their backslidings." Observe, God's mercy can reclaim the persecutor; it can soften the impenitent; it can bring back some who are gone astray. Mercy can destroy the sins of the nation and yet save the nation. It is a healing mercy. "I will heal their backslidings." These are the sparks that God causes to arise.

OBJECTION. But things still look and seem as if they are in the dark. We would have more light. What must we do? How must we carry ourselves till God makes light to arise to us in darkness?

ANSWER 1. Let us, in all dark providences, go into our chambers. Isaiah 26:20: "Come my people, enter thou into thy chamber, and hide thyself." Enter into your chamber, that is, we must go and search our hearts by serious meditation. Go into this chamber of your hearts. Let us, in the first place, search our evidences for heaven, bring our graces to the touchstone. Let us see what faith we have and what love for God we have.

Does conscience witness that we not only serve God but love Him? Can we cry out for God, for the living God? Are we carried up to heaven in a fiery chariot of love? Is it thus with us? Oh, let us search into the chambers of our hearts and see how all things stand between God and our souls!

My brethren, when things are dark without, we need to have all clear within.

Let us go not only into the chamber of our hearts, but let us go into the chamber of divine promises, and there let us judge ourselves a while. Oh, these sweet promises of God which our souls may take comfort in! God has promised comfort to all His mourners. God has promised that He will strengthen the infirmed, Isaiah 40:29. God has promised a crown of glory, Revelation 2:10. He has said that He will never leave us nor forsake us. Let us now, by faith, hide ourselves in these chambers. That's the first thing we are to do.

ANSWER 2. Having done this, let us, under all clouds of darkness, in the next place commit ourselves to God so that He would safeguard and keep us. This I ground upon that Scripture in Psalm 37:5: "Commit thy way unto the Lord." In the Hebrew it is "roll thy way upon the Lord." Commit yourself and your cause to God by prayer. As an orphan commits himself under care of his guardian, so should we give all our care to God. "Commit thy way unto the Lord." Let us do our duty and trust God with our safety. It is our work to cast care; it is God's work to take care.

ANSWER 3. Having gone into these chambers, the chambers of our hearts and the chambers of divine promises, now, in the third place, let us now wait for God's time till He shall make light to arise in our horizon, until God turns our darkness into the light of the morning. God can suddenly disperse the black clouds. God can create light; God can strike a straight stroke by a crooked stick; God can remove the mountains that lie in our way till light arises.

Let us patiently wait; light will spring up. The blessings that we expectat are worth waiting for. To see the golden fleet of prayer come laden home with rich returns of mercy, to see peace and truth united, to see popery and profaneness abominated, to see the beauty of holiness shining forth like a lamp that burns, to see Christ ride in triumph in the chariot of His gospel, to see the righteous honored and renowned and be like the wings of a dove covered with yellow gold—these certainly are mercies worth waiting for. Therefore, let us wait patiently.

And to encourage holy waiting, I will shut up all with that Scripture, Isaiah 30:18: "And therefore will the Lord wait, that He may be gracious unto you; and therefore will He be exalted, that He may have mercy upon you; for the Lord is a God of judgment; blessed are all they that wait for Him."

The Good Shepherd

"I am the good Shepherd, and know My sheep, and am known of Mine." John 10:14

Every line of Scripture has majesty shining in it. Jesus Christ is the very center of the gospel. If the Scripture is the field, Christ is the pearl in this field; and blessed is he who finds this pearl. The Scripture gives various descriptions of Christ. Sometimes He is called a Physician; He is the great Healer of souls; sometimes He is called a Captain. Hebrews 2:10: "Captain of our salvation." And here in the text He is a shepherd: "I am the good Shepherd." And this Shepherd has a flock; so it is in the text: "I know My sheep, and am known of Mine." These sheep are the elect company of believers; these are His rational sheep. First, I shall speak of the sheep, then something of the Shepherd as they relate to one another.

Concerning the sheep: "I know My sheep." The wicked are compared to goats, the saints to sheep. Christ's people are His sheep, and there are some analogies between them.

First, a sheep is an innocent creature. It is not hurtful or ravenous, as other creatures are, but is very harmless and inoffensive. So those sheep who belong to Christ, and are of His fold, are innocent. Philippians 2:15: "That you may be blameless," that you may be harmless. The Greek word is "without horn," or

"without pushing or horning"—that you may be harmless. Christ's people walk as nearly as they can so that
they may give no just offense. They would rather suffer
wrong than do wrong. Those who are set upon mis-
chief are not Christ's sheep but are birds of prey.
Those who would plot the ruin of a kingdom and spill
Protestant blood are none of Christ's sheep. These are
wolves who have been suckled with the milk of the
Romish whore. These are goats whom Christ will set at
His left hand, Matthew 25:32.

Second, a sheep is noted for meekness in Scripture;
it is a meek creature. Let the shearer take its wool, it
does not resist. If you strike a sheep, it does not snarl
or fly in your face. All Christ's sheep are meek-spirited,
2 Samuel 16:12. Though a child of God may sometimes
fall into a froward fit, yet he grieves for it and weeps for
his unmortified passion.

Third, a sheep is a clean creature; it is neat and
cleanly; it delights most in pure streams and clean pastures. So Christ's sheep are clean and sanctified; holiness is the thing they pray for. Psalm 51:10: "Create in
me a clean heart, O God!" Though they are not perfectly holy, yet they are perfecting holiness in the fear
of God. They are neat creatures, and would rather die
than go through dirty, miry places. So it is with Christ's
sheep—they will suffer anything rather than defile
their conscience. Genesis 39:9: "How can I do this
wickedness and sin against God?"

The wicked in Scripture are compared to swine.
They wallow in sin, in their wickedness and uncleanness. They are steeped and boiled in sin. Aye, but a
good Christian breathes after sanctity. A child of God
may fall into sin unawares, as did David, but he does

not lie in sin. He recovers himself again by repentance. A sheep may fall into the mire, but it does not lie there; it gets out again.

Fourth, a sheep is a very useful creature. There is nothing about it that is not of some use—the flesh, the fleece, the skin. So all Christ's sheep, who are the sheep of His pasture, are useful. They are still doing good, they are profitable to others by their knowledge, counsel, example, prayers, and good works. They are useful in their places. The wicked are compared to wood, Ezekiel 15:3, which is good for nothing but fuel. Sinners are useless; their life is scarcely worth a prayer, nor their death scarcely worth a tear. They live to encumber the ground. But God's people are useful; they are called the excellent of the earth, Psalm 16:3. They are blessings in the places where they come.

Fifth, a sheep is a very contented creature. It will feed upon any pasture where you put it. Put sheep upon the bare common and they are content. They feed upon the little they pick up in the fallow ground, a perfect emblem of true saints who are the sheep of Christ. Let God put them into what pasture He will and they are content, Philippians 4:11. They have learned in every state therewith to be content. Paul could want or abound. He could be anything that God wanted him to be. He was content with that portion, whatever it was, that providence carved out to him.

You who are apt to murmur and repine at your condition, and think you never have enough, think to yourselves: Sheep are content with their pasture; surely were I one of Christ's sheep I would be content. You who have the least of the world, you have more than you know how to be thankful for. He who has the least bit of bread will die in God's debt. A sheep is a contented creature.

Sixth, to name no more, a sheep is a timorous creature. It is very fearful if any danger approaches, or if it is frightened by the wolf. Thus the saints of God, who are Christ's sheep, pass the time of their sojourning here in fear. They are fearful of provoking God, of wounding their peace, fearful of temptation, fearful they should come short of heaven through sloth, Hebrews 4:1. It is an earmark of Christ's sheep that they are endued with the fear of God, Genesis 42:28. This is their earmark, men fearing God. It's true, the righteous are as bold as a lion in a righteous cause, but timorous and fearful of sinful fear. And, let me tell you, happy is he who in this sense fears always. Holy fear is the best antidote against temptation. The way to be safe is always to fear.

To make some use of this, let us all labor to be found in the number of Christ's sheep. All the world is divided into two ranks—sheep and goats. If you would be glad to be found in the day of judgment as Christ's sheep, and sit at His right hand, be much in prayer. Pray to God that He would change your nature, that He would take away your wolfish nature, your fierceness, your frowardness, and that He would transform you into His own image. Labor to be among Christ's sheep, to get into Christ's fold.

There is only one way in which you do not want to be like sheep, for sheep are apt to wander sometimes from their fold. Take heed that you do not straggle into bypaths of error and heresy. It is dangerous to wander for fear the devil, the wolf, should catch you. Don't go astray as sheep; but in other things resemble sheep in meekness, in patience, in usefulness, in willingness.

And particularly in this one thing let us labor to resemble sheep: when the shepherd's dog comes near, all the sheep flock together. Persecution should be like the shepherd's dog. It should make all Christ's sheep run together and unite. Do Papists and Formalists agree in persecuting God's people? And shall not the saints of God agree to keep the unity of the Spirit in the bond of peace? Love is the earmark by which Christ's sheep are known. John 13:35: "By this shall all men know ye are My disciples, if ye love one another." It was the harlot who said, "Let the child be divided." It is the Jesuit who says, "Let the Church of God be divided." It is Satan's great design to set his cloven foot among God's people to make division and contention among the sons of Zion. The devil's best music is discord.

Oh! Let all Christ's people, His sheep, flock together and associate in love. Those who hope to meet together in heaven should not fall out by the way. Unity is the great music in heaven. There is unity in the Trinity, and unity among saints would be a great blessing on earth. For Christians to unite is their interest and wisdom; union is their strength, union is their glory and their ornament. This was the honor of the primitive churches, all of one heart, Acts 2:1. There was but one heart among them. Let the sheep of Christ unite together. When the saints are harmoniously united, then they adorn their blessed Shepherd, the Lord Jesus. So much for the first of these: Christ's sheep.

Second, to speak something of the shepherd. "I am the good Shepherd." This is as true an epithet as ever was given. Zechariah 13:7: "A good Shepherd." 1 Peter 2:5: "You are now returned to the Shepherd and Bishop of your souls." Your conscience is the diocese where none may visit but Christ. Christ is called in Scripture "the chief Shepherd of all," 1 Peter 5:4. Ministers are but shepherds under Him to look to His flock. Christ is the chief Shepherd. So, then, the observation is this:

DOCTRINE. Jesus Christ is the blessed Shepherd of His sheep.

In Scripture, Christ is called the great Shepherd and the good Shepherd. He is called the great Shepherd in Hebrews 13:20-21, and here in the text He is called the good Shepherd. Christ is the great Shepherd, since He made the sheep, and He is the good Shepherd since He saves His sheep. So, you see, He is both the great and the good Shepherd. There are many parallels and analogies between Christ and His sheep. I will state some of them.

1. *A shepherd is appointed to his calling.* Why, so Christ is the true Shepherd who entered in by the door. John 10:2: "He entered in by the door." What's the meaning of that? It is that Christ is lawfully called and appointed to His keeping of the sheep.

2. *A shepherd knows his flock, knows all his flock.* This is in the text: "I am the good Shepherd, I know My sheep," said Christ. Christ's knowing His sheep implies a knowledge of approbation. Christ's knowing His sheep is His loving them. This is a great consolation, that Christ knows all His sheep. He knows every one of their names. John 10:3: "He calleth His own sheep by

name." He knows all the sighs and groans they make. Psalm 38:9: "My groaning is not hid from Thee." Christ knows every tear they shed. He bottles their tears as wine. Psalm 56:8: "Put Thou my tears into Thy bottle." He knows all their sufferings. Judges 10:16: "His soul was pierced for the miseries of Israel." Christ knows all their good works, all their works of piety and charity, and will shortly say, "Come ye blessed of My Father, inherit the kingdom." What a comfort is this! Christ knows all His sheep by name.

3. *A shepherd marks his sheep that he may distinguish them from other strange sheep.* So Jesus Christ, this blessed Shepherd, sets a double mark upon His sheep. One is the earmark of election. "I have chosen you," He said; and besides that he has set another mark upon His sheep. He seals them by His Spirit, Ephesians 4:30. The sanctifying graces are the several badges and seals that Christ puts upon His sheep. How will this raise the saints' triumph in heaven! How will this make them bless God that they should be marked out as sheep when most of the world are marked as goats!

4. *A shepherd seeks his sheep when they are lost and gone astray, Luke 15:4.* That is the office of the shepherd— he seeks his sheep. Let me assure you, Christ's sheep are lost naturally. They have strayed far from the fold and are so lost that they can never find their way home of themselves. A dog or a horse, if lost, can find the way home again, but if a sheep is lost it can never find its way home. This is the case of lapsed souls. They are so lost that they cannot find their way.

Now Jesus Christ, this blessed Shepherd, seeks these lost sheep. He left His Father's bosom. He came from heaven on purpose to seek His lost, wandering sheep. Luke 19:10: "The Son of Man is come to seek and to save that which was lost." Zaccheus was a lost sheep, a great sinner, an extortioner. This lost sheep was found upon a sycamore tree. There Christ saw him and called him. Luke 19:5: "Zaccheus, make haste and come down." Christ entered first into Zaccheus' heart and then He entered into his house: "This day is salvation come to this house."

There may be some who are as yet lost sheep. They have wandered from God and have gone on in the ways of sin. But if they belong to this good Shepherd, if they belong to Christ, He will at one time or another bring home these wandering sheep by converting grace.

5. *A shepherd leads and guides his sheep.* And thus Christ, this blessed Shepherd, guides His people that they should not go wrong. John 10:3: "He leads them out." How does Christ guide His people? He guides them with His eye; His eye is never off of them, though their eye is too much off from Him. Psalm 32:8: "Thou shalt guide me with Thine eye." That is, "The eye of Thy providence shall direct me."

Again, Christ guides His people by the oracle of His holy Word. Psalm 73:24: "Thou shalt guide me with Thy counsel." And Christ guides His people by the sweet conduct of His Spirit. John 16:13: "He will guide you into all truth; when the Spirit of truth is come unto you, He will guide you into all truth." Besides, Christ appoints ministers to be guides. If Christ's sheep go out of the way, His ministers are appointed to bring them back again to the fold.

6. *A shepherd governs his sheep.* They have as much need of governing as guiding. He governs his sheep;

he orders them and brings them into a decorum. So the Lord Jesus governs His people. Christ's pastoral staff is a type and emblem of His governing the saints. Isaiah 9:6: "The government shall be upon His shoulder." Christ's sheep are apt sometimes to be disorderly. They are apt to slight their shepherd, to grow wanton, to despise their pastor, to quarrel one with another. But now Jesus Christ, this blessed Shepherd, has His laws to bind them, and He has His shepherd's rod to rule them. He brings them into good order. We want as well Christ's rod to govern us as His blood to save us.

7. *A shepherd relieves and feeds his sheep by the way.* He won't see them starve. The Greek word for shepherd signifies to feed. The Lord Jesus mercifully feeds His flock. He won't let them starve. Isaiah 40:11: "He shall feed His flock like a shepherd." Christ feeds His people in the sanctuary. God's tables are this Shepherd's tents. Every ordinance is a fresh pasture for the saints to feed in. Christ feeds souls with the Bread of Life. He fed them with that spiritual supper at His own table. Here is the love of Christ, the great Shepherd of souls: He provides plenty of pasture. Though some would rob Christ's sheep of their green pastures and starve them, yet Christ will feed them. As long as Christ has a spiritual flock of sheep in the world, He will rather work a miracle than allow them not to be provided for. "He shall feed His flock like a shepherd."

8. *A shepherd makes it a part of his work to look after his sick sheep.* Christ's sheep are apt to be sick—some sick of pride, some sick of discontent, some sick of envy, and some sick of covetousness. Christ's sheep are apt to be sick, and He cures all His sheep so that they shall

never die of the rot. Ezekiel 34:16: "I will bind up that
which is broken, I will strengthen that which is sick."
Christ has those sovereign oils and balsams that can
cure the worst distemper. He has appointed the
preaching of the Word to be a healer of sin-sick souls,
Ezekiel 47. The Word preached is like the waters of the
sanctuary, both for food and for medicine.

9. *A shepherd keeps a continual watch over his flock that
they are not stolen or devoured by the wolf.* So Christ
watches over His flock by His omniscience so that no
hurt comes to His elect, so that they are not infected by
sin and ensnared by temptation. Christ has His
shepherd's eyes to watch His flock, and He has His
shepherd's staff to beat off the wolf.

10. *A shepherd has compassion on his sheep.* So Jesus
Christ has tender emotions for all His elect. Isaiah
40:11: "He shall gather the lambs in His arms, and
carry them in His bosom, and gently lead those that
are with young." Christ Jesus is tender with His lambs.
He puts them in His bosom, and such as are weak and
ready to faint He gently leads. Oh, the bowels of compassion of Christ to the elect! He is full of sympathy.
The lambs never cry but their cries go to Christ's heart.
Therefore in Scripture Christ is said to be touched
with the feeling of their infirmities, Hebrews 4:5. The
saints never bleed but Christ bleeds in their wounds.
Isaiah 63:9: "In all their afflictions He was afflicted."

Thus much, as briefly as I could, you have the
analogies and parallels between Christ and the shepherd. He is the Shepherd of His flock.

How Christ is a Better Shepherd

In the second place, I shall show you how Christ is better than any other shepherd, and infinitely excels and transcends them, as it appears in these particulars:

1. *Christ is a better Shepherd than any other in respect of the glory and dignity of His person.* They are of the earth, earthly, but Christ is a Shepherd from heaven; He is of divine origin. He is equal with God the Father, Philippians 2:6. He has a consubstantiality with God the Father.

2. *Christ excels other shepherds in that He cleanses and purifies His flock.* Revelation 1:5, Christ "washeth us from our sins in His own blood." While Christ's sheep are in the world they will be apt to get spots, for the world is good for nothing but to spot—one spotted with pride, another spotted with earthliness. Oh, how the people of God deface God's image by rubbing it against the earth! And the truth is, going too much among the goats defiles them. But now Jesus Christ cleanses and purifies His flock and washes away their spots. Christ's sheep are white and washed in the blood of the Lamb.

3. *Christ excels all other shepherds in that He has an art that no other shepherds have: He teaches His sheep.* Other shepherds guide their sheep but they cannot teach them. But Christ teaches His sheep who belong to His fold of election. He instructs them in the mysteries of salvation, and He teaches them after the most excellent manner—He teaches like God.

(1) Christ so teaches all His sheep that He makes them willing to learn. Psalm 110:3: "They shall be a willing people." Christ not only informs the judgment,

but inclines the will to embrace the truth and makes them willing to learn.

(2) Christ not only teaches the ear, but He teaches the heart. Acts 16:14: "Lydia, whose heart the Lord opened."

(3) Christ teaches His sheep not only to understand, but He teaches them to obey. Isaiah 2:3: "He will teach us of His ways, and we will go in them." So Christ teaches His sheep after the most excellent manner—He makes them docile.

4. *Jesus Christ is a better Shepherd than any on earth was before or after because Christ prays for His sheep;* many shepherds scarcely pray for themselves. Christ prays for all His elect sheep. John 17:9: "I will pray for them." As Christ knows every sheep by name, so Christ prays for every sheep by name. "I pray for them." And what does Christ pray for them? Why, He prays that they may not wander, that they may not tire or faint, that they may not die by the way. And this is Christ's prayer for His sheep, John 17:11: "Holy Father, keep them whom Thou hast given Me." And this prayer of Christ's prevails with God. If we consider Christ either in His office or in His relation to God, His prayer must be prevalent. Consider Him in His office as He is a Priest; consider Him as He is in relation, as He is a Son. If God could forget Christ as a Priest, yet He could not forget Christ as His Son. John 11:42: "I knew Thou always hearest Me." And this prayer of Christ for His elect sheep is perpetuated. There is not one minute wherein we can say that Christ is not praying for us. How can these sheep miscarry when their blessed Shepherd is always watching over them and praying for them?

5. *Jesus Christ is a better Shepherd than any other in that*

He shows more dear affection and tender love to His sheep than any shepherd in this world ever did. And no wonder Christ should thus love His sheep. Because they are His own He has a propriety in them. In John 10:27 He calls them "My sheep." A man may be a shepherd when he is not owner of the flock of sheep. A hireling may take charge of the sheep when, perhaps, he never cared for the sheep, John 10:13. But Christ is the owner of the sheep. Though the pope blasphemously calls himself the Head of the Church, and lords it over Christ's flocks, yet the pope is a usurper. The Lord Jesus is the right owner of His sheep, and hence it follows that Christ has such dear affection and tender love for these sheep, because they are His own.

Now, that Christ bears more love to His sheep than any other shepherd ever did appears in these three particulars: (1) He treats His sheep with compassion; (2) He comforts His sheep; and (3) He died for His sheep. Was there ever any love parallel to this?

(1) Christ treats all His sheep with compassion, and I ground this upon that previously cited Scripture in Isaiah 40:11: "He shall gather the lambs in His arms, and carry them in His bosom, and gently lead those that are with young." Christ, you see, is tender of His lambs and puts them in His bosom near His heart; and such as are faint He gently leads. Oh, the mercies of Christ to His elect sheep! That's the first point, Christ loves His sheep and treats them with compassion. His heart yearns over them.

(2) Christ not only treats His sheep with compassion, but He comforts them. The people of Christ who are His sheep are given to trembling. Sheep are trembling, fearful creatures, and are apt to be discour-

aged. Now Christ comforts and revives them. Isaiah 12:1: "Thou comfortedst me." Christ comforts His people in two ways:

First, Christ comforts them in the use of ordinances—Word and Sacrament. In the one we hear Christ's voice, in the other we have His kiss and embraces. In the use of gospel ordinances the saints are oftentimes upon the Mount of Transfiguration. They feed upon holy liquid. Christ gives them suddenly such inward revivings as carry them above the love of life and the fear of death.

Second, Christ comforts His people, the flock of His pasture, by His Spirit, who is called the Comforter in John 14:16. The Spirit enables us to work out our adoption, to read our names in the promises. The Spirit seals up God's love to the heart, upon which there is a current of divine joy running into the soul. Here is Christ's love to His sheep—He comforts them.

(3) Christ shows His love to His elect sheep in that He shed His blood for them. John 10:11: "I lay down My life for My sheep." The death of the Shepherd is the life of the sheep. Consider Christ's death in a threefold notion: it was painful; it was voluntary; and it was meritorious. In all these ways He shows His love in dying for His sheep.

First, look upon Christ's death as painful. If the torment of the body was so great, oh, what was the agony of the soul! The Lord Jesus Christ was trodden. He was squeezed in the winepress of His Father's wrath. The evangelists use three words worthy of observing to express Christ's agony. The text says He began to be amazed, He began to faint, and He began to be exceedingly sorrowful, Matthew 26:37. He felt hell's torment in His soul, equivalent, though not locally. Though Christ was anointed with the Holy Ghost, though He was supported with the Deity, though He was comforted with angels from heaven, yet for all that He sweated great drops of blood, the text says. Oh, the love of Christ in dying for His sheep!

Second, consider Christ's death as voluntary. He parted with His life freely. It is true, Christ's death was necessary with regard to God's decree, but it was voluntary in the respect that Christ cheerfully yielded to suffering. John 10:18: "I lay down My life." The Jews could not have taken away His life if He had not laid it down. Nothing could have forced Christ to have died for His sheep but love. Nothing could have bound Him to the cross but the golden chain of love.

Third, consider Christ's death as meritorious. It is the inlet to all holy benediction; it procures for us justification of our persons, acceptance of our services, and access to the throne of grace. It procures an entrance into the holy, acceptable place of heaven, Hebrews 3:19. Behold, here is the love of Christ in laying down His life for His sheep. He has purchased glorious things for us. There was no way for the sheep to live but by the death of the Shepherd. And for Christ Jesus to die as a malefactor, having the weight of so many sins lying upon Him, was more than if all the angels had been turned into dust.

6. *Christ is a better Shepherd than any other in that He can make all the care and pains He takes with His sheep to be successful, which no other shepherd can do.* Other shepherds may lead the sheep to water or to pasture, but they cannot make the sheep have a stomach. They cannot make them have an appetite; they cannot make

the pasture nourish the sheep. But Christ, our blessed
Shepherd, as He leads His sheep into the pasture, so
He can cause an appetite in His sheep for their food.
He can make them, by speaking a word, hunger and
thirst after righteousness. Jesus Christ provides pastures for His sheep, and He alone can bless these pastures and make them nourishing to the soul. 1
Timothy 4:6: "Nourished up in the words of faith."
Christ can bless the blessed Sacrament. He can make
the elements, through the operation of His Spirit, to
be spiritual growth and nourishment in His elect
sheep. Thus He is a better Shepherd—He can bless the
pasture.

7. *Christ is a better Shepherd than any other in the world
for He is a pattern and example to all His flock—an example
of meekness, humility, and sanctity.* He is a pattern for all
His flock, and in this sense observe that Christ is said to
go before His sheep, John 10:34. How did He go before them? By His holy example. 1 Peter 2:21: "For
even hereunto were ye called, because Christ also suffered for us, leaving us an example, that ye should follow in His steps."

Jerome, having read the religious life of Delyan,
and what an excellent end he made, said, "Delyan shall
be the example I will follow." So let all the sheep of
Christ say, "Jesus Christ shall be the example that we
will follow and imitate." Christ's sheep go astray when
they do not tread in the steps of their Shepherd, the
Lord Jesus.

8. *Christ Jesus is a better Shepherd than any other, and
far excels them, in that He keeps His sheep so fast in His
hands that none can ever pluck them out.* John 10:28:
"Neither can any man pluck them out of My hand."

Not one of Christ's sheep was ever lost. Though a shepherd is never so careful and vigilant, yet sometimes a sheep may go astray and be devoured by the wolf; but not one of Christ's elect sheep was ever lost. John 17:12: "Not one of them is lost, but the son of perdition." Judas was never given to Christ; he was not a sheep but a goat. None of His sheep was ever lost.

Christ's sheep may sometimes go astray by error, and may fall into the acts of sin as did David, but Christ will reduce them and bring them off again by speedy repentance. Christ's sheep may be lame and faint, and can hardly go, but Christ cares for the weak sheep as well as the strong sheep. The bruised reed He will not break. The weakest saint alive is so much a sheep that he is part of his Shepherd. Christ and believers are one. The sheep cannot perish without the Shepherd perishing likewise.

9. *Christ is a better Shepherd than any other in that He puts His sheep into a better pasture at last.* He takes them out of the wilderness here, the valley of tears, and transplants them into paradise, there to feed among the lilies. He gives them eternal life. John 10:28: "I give unto them eternal life." Christ's sheep may lose their golden fleece; men may rob them of their wool; and they may lose their lives for Christ's sake, aye, but Christ gives them eternal life. Life is sweet, but that word "eternal" makes it far sweeter. Eternal life consists in the fruition of all good things—life, beauty, strength, joy, perfection, and eternity. Here is the excellency of our good Shepherd—He gives His sheep eternal life. He will take them out of the wilderness, where there are fiery serpents, and place them in paradise where they shall feed among the cherubims.

Thus I have shown you how the Lord Jesus resembles a shepherd, and how He is a better Shepherd than any other. Give me leave now to make some application.

USE 1. Is the Lord Jesus Christ this great Shepherd who takes such care for His flock, and is He a better Shepherd than any other? Then let us all labor to know our Shepherd. Here in the text Christ says, "I know My sheep: and I know them by name." Aye, and He is known of them too. Oh, let us know our blessed Shepherd. Knowing Christ is nothing else but believing in Him. In Scripture, knowledge is sometimes put for faith. Isaiah 53:11: "By His knowledge shall My righteous Servant justify many." Knowledge is there put for faith. Then do we know our Shepherd, Christ, when we believe in Him.

The blind world is ignorant of Christ. John 17:25: "The world hath not known Me." No? When they heard Christ preach? They saw His miracles, but neither oracle nor miracle would work upon them. Christ said, "The world hath not known Me." Formalists do not know Christ savingly. They have light but they lack sight, as if the sun should shine upon a blind eye. We know Christ aright when we believe in Him, when we fetch virtue from Him, and then we are transformed into His likeness. This is to know Christ. Oh, let us never rest till we know the Bishop and Shepherd of our souls, the Lord Jesus.

As our comfort lies in Christ knowing us, so it lies in our knowing Christ. Our comfort lies in Christ's knowing us with a knowledge of approbation, and also in our knowing Christ with a knowledge of apprehension. That's the first use: let us know our Shepherd. Such as do not know Christ will hear Christ say to them, "I never knew you."

USE 2. Let us not only know our Shepherd, but let us hearken to the voice of our blessed Shepherd, our Lord Jesus. As soon as ever the shepherd comes into the field, the sheep know his voice. Oh, let us hear Christ's voice! John 10:27: "My sheep hear My voice." Christ's voice is in the preaching of the Word. Therefore observe that Christ is said now, just now, to speak from heaven to us, Hebrews 12:25. How does He speak now from heaven but in the preaching of the Word? Oh, then, hear Christ speak. But take heed, don't hear the voice of a stranger, John 10:5. Christ said that they would not follow a stranger. Sheep will not follow a stranger. By stranger is meant one who is heterodox and would bring strange wonders into the Church and poison Christ's sheep. As you must hearken to Christ's voice, so take heed that you don't listen to the voice of a stranger.

Christ's sheep are rational. He has given them a spirit of discerning, and they are able by their wisdom to distinguish between truth and error. They will not hear the voice of a stranger. We must hear Christ's voice, but when do we hear Christ's voice aright? We hear Christ's voice aright when we obey His voice, and never until then. In John 10, and several other places, you read of obeying the voice of Christ. When Christ speaks of self-denial, of meekness and mercifulness, we obey Him and are ambitious to obey Him. A good Christian is like the flower that opens with the sun—he opens to Christ's commands; he cordially obeys

Christ's. This is to hear Christ's voice.

USE 3. If Christ is the great, blessed, and good
Shepherd, then let us all labor to evidence to ourselves
that we belong to this Shepherd, that we are the sheep
of Christ's pasture. Let us search and try whether or
not we have the earmark of Christ's sheep, whether we
are like sheep. A sheep is a pure and clean creature.
Are we like the sheep of Christ? Are our hearts
cleansed from all filthiness of flesh and spirit? He who
lies wallowing in sin is a swine, not a sheep.

A sheep is a very useful creature. Everything in a
sheep is good for something. The milk, the flesh, the
fleece, everything is useful. Are we the sheep of Christ?
Are we useful? We should be always doing good; this is
the very end of our living, to be good and do good.
How useful was St. Paul? The care of all the churches
lay upon him.

USE 4. Is Christ this blessed Shepherd better than
any other shepherd? Oh, then, let us labor to love and
honor this blessed Shepherd! Does the Shepherd die
for His sheep, and shall not the sheep love their
Shepherd? Those who do not love Christ are not sheep
but goats. Give Christ, I beseech you, the best of your
love, the cream of your love. The spouse gave Christ
the juice of her pomegranate, Song of Solomon 8:2,
her spiced wine.

Love Christ better than estate or relations.
Relations may lie in our bosoms, but Christ must lie in
our hearts. Our love to the Lord Jesus must be intent
and ardent. We should, like seraphims, burn in a holy
flame of love for Christ. If a man had three souls, as a

philosopher once dreamed, they would all be too little for Christ. Let us so love Christ, and show it, by an open acknowledgment of Christ if we are called to it. This is love, to dare to own Christ, our blessed Shepherd. It is said of the chief rulers, John 12:42, that they believed on Christ but did not confess Him lest they should be put out of the synagogue. Christ will never own that faith which will never entertain Christ. He who is ashamed of Christ is a shame to Christ.

USE 5. I will but name it. Let us answer all the love and cost of Christ, our blessed Shepherd. How should we answer this cost? By holy fruitfulness. 1 Corinthians 9:7: "Who feedeth a flock, and eateth not the milk of the flock?" Christ has feasted you as His flock. Christ has feasted you with His body and blood. Oh, then, feast Him with the fruits of righteousness; be fruitful in knowledge; be fruitful in good works.

I will close all with Song of Solomon 4:2: "Thy teeth are like a flock of sheep that are even shorn, which came up from the washing, whereof every one bear twins, and none is barren among them."

How Must We Make Religion Our Business?

"Wist ye not that I must be about My Father's business?" Luke 2:49

These are the words of our Lord Jesus, whose lips dropped as a honeycomb. The occasion was this: Christ, having the Spirit of wisdom and sanctity poured out upon Him without measure, being but 12 years old, went to the temple and fell to disputing with the doctors, verse 46. Where should learning blossom but upon that tree which bore several sorts of fruit? Who could better interpret secrets than He who lay in His Father's bosom, Colossians 2:9? According to Luke 2:47, "All that heard Him were astonished at His understanding." In the Greek it is "they were out of themselves" with admiration. Well might they admire that He who had never been at the university should be able to silence the great rabbis. John 7:15: "How knoweth this man letters, having never learned?"

While they were wondering, his mother, who now was come to seek Him, propounded this question: "Son, why hast Thou thus dealt with us?" Luke 2:48. That is, "Why hast Thou put us to all this labor in seeking Thee?" In the words of the text, Christ made a rational and religious reply: "Wist ye not that I must be about My Father's business?" In the Greek it is "in the

things of My Father." It is as if Christ had said, "I must
be doing the work which My Father in heaven has set
Me about; for this I received My mission and unction,
that I might do the will of Him who sent Me." What am
I in the world for but to promote His glory, propagate
His truth, and be as a magnet to draw souls to heaven?
"Wist ye not that I must be about My Father's busi-
ness?"

From this example of our blessed Savior in making
His Father's work His business, we learn this great
truth:

**DOCTRINE. It is the duty of every Christian to
make religion his business.**

Religion is not a sometime thing, only secondary in
importance, or the thing "by the by," proper only for
spare hours; but it must be the grand business of our
lives. St. Paul made it so. His great care was to know
Christ and be found in Christ, Philippians 3:9-10. How
abundantly did he lay himself out for God! "I labored
more abundantly than they all," 1 Corinthians 15:10.
St. Paul moved heavenward, not slowly as the dial on
the sun but as the sun in its hemisphere, with a winged
swiftness. He made religion his business.

For the illustrating and unfolding of this, there are
three questions to be resolved:

1. What is meant by religion?
2. Why must we make religion our business?
3. What is it to make religion our business?

QUESTION 1. What is meant by religion?

ANSWER. The Latin word signifies a knitting together. Sin has loosened us from God, but when religion comes into the heart it fastens the heart to God

again, as the members are knit to the head by several
nerves and ligaments. Religion is the spiritual sinew
and ligament that knits us to God. The Greek word for
religion signifies a right worshipping. This is religion,
when we not only worship the true God, but in that
manner which He has prescribed—by a right rule,
from a right principle, and to a right end.

QUESTION 2. Why must we make religion our
business?
ANSWER. Because religion is a matter of the highest nature. While we are serving God we are doing
angels' work. The business of religion infinitely out-
balances all other things besides. Pleasure, profit, and
honor (the trinity which the world adores) are all of an
inferior alloy and must give way to religion. The fear of
God is said to be the whole duty of man, Ecclesiastes
12:13; or, as it is in the Hebrew, the whole of man.
Other things may delight; religion satiates. Other
things may make us wise to admiration; religion makes
us wise to salvation, 2 Timothy 3:15.

QUESTION 3. What is it to make religion our
business?
ANSWER. It consists principally in these seven
things:
1. *We make religion our business when we wholly devote
ourselves to religion.* Psalm 119:38: "Establish Thy Word
unto Thy servant, who is devoted to Thy fear." We must
be as the scholar who devotes himself to his studies
and makes learning his business. A godly man may
sometimes run himself, through rashness and thought-
lessness, upon that which is evil. There is no man so

bad but he may do some good actions; and there is no man so good but he may do some bad actions. But the course and tenor of a godly man's life is religious. When he deviates to sin, yet he devotes himself to God. It is with Christians as it is with a company of mariners at sea. They are bound for some coast, and may meet with such a crosswind as may turn them back and drive them in a quite contrary way. But as soon as the storm is over and the sea calm, they recover themselves again and get into the right way where they sailed before. So it is with a Christian. Heaven is the haven he is bound for; the Scripture is the compass he sails by; yet, by a contrary wind of temptation blowing, he may be driven back into a sinful action. But he recovers himself again by repentance and sails on constantly to the heavenly port. This is to make religion our business, when, notwithstanding some excursions through human frailty, we are devoted to God's fear and dedicate our entire existence to God.

2. *We make religion our business when we devote much attention to the business of religion chiefly.* It gains the pre-eminence. "Seek ye first the kingdom of God," Matthew 6:33; first in time, before all things, and first in affection, above all things. We must give religion the precedence, making all other things either subservient or subordinate to it. We are to provide for our families, but chiefly for our souls. This is to make religion our business. Jacob put the cattle before and made his wives and children lag after, Genesis 32:16. It is unworthy to make religion come behind in the rear. It must lead the van, and all other things must stoop and bow to it. He never had religion in his heart who said to any worldly thing, "In the throne, you shall be greater."

3. *We make religion our business when our thoughts are most busied about religion.* While others are thinking what they shall do to get a living, our thoughts are what we shall do to be saved. David mused upon God: "While I was musing, the fire burned," Psalm 39:3. Thoughts are as passengers in the soul. When we travel every day to the city of God and are contemplating glory and eternity, this is to make religion our business. Theophylact calls holy contemplation "the gate and portal by which we enter into heaven." A Christian, by divine soliloquies and ejaculations, is in heaven before his time. He is wrapped up into paradise; his thoughts are all packed up and gone.

4. *We make religion our business when our main end and scope is to serve God.* He is said to make the world his busness whose great design is to get the world. Paul's ultimate end was that Christ might be magnified and the church edified. Our aims must be good as well as our actions. Many make use of religion for sinister ends, like the eagle; while she flies aloft, her eye is upon her prey. Hypocrites serve God on account of other advantages. They love the temple for the gold; they court the gospel not for its beauty, but for its jewels. These do not make religion their business, but a political trick and artifice to get money. But then we make religion our business when the glory of God is mainly in our eye, and the very purport and intent of our life is to live to Him who hath died for us. God is the center, and all the lines of our actions must be drawn to this center.

5. *We make religion our business when we trade with God every day.* "Our conversation is in heaven," Philippians 3:20. The Greek word for "conversation" signifies

commerce and traffic. Our merchandise is in heaven. A man may live in one place and drive his trade in another. Though a saint lives in the world, yet he trades above the moon. He is a merchant for the pearl of price. This is to make religion our business. When we keep a holy intercourse with God, there is a trade driven between us and heaven. "Our fellowship is with the Father, and with His Son Jesus Christ," 1 John 1:3. God comes down to us upon the wing of His Spirit, and we go up to Him upon the wing of prayer.

6. *We make religion our business when we redeem time from secular things for the service of God.* A good Christian is the greatest monopolizer. He hoards up all the time he can for religion. Psalm 119:62: "At midnight I will rise to give thanks to Thee." Those are the best hours which are spent with God. David, having tasted how sweet the Lord was, would borrow some time from his sleep that he might take a turn in heaven. It well becomes Christians to take time from worldly occasions, sinful dressings, idle visits, that they may be the more intent upon the matters of religion.

I have read of a holy man who, being tempted by his former evil companions to sin, made this answer: "I am so busy in reading a little book with three leaves that I have no leisure so much as to mind my other business." And being asked afterward whether he had read over the book, he replied, "This book with three leaves is of three colors—red, white, and black—which contain such deep mysteries that I have resolved with myself to read therein all the days of my life. In the first leaf, which is red, I meditate on the precious blood of Christ which was shed for my sins. In the white leaf, I meditate on the pure and delicious joys of heaven. In the black leaf, I contemplate the hideous and dreadful torments of hell, prepared for the wicked to all eternity."

This is to make religion our business, when we are so taken up with it that we have scarcely any leisure for other things. Christian, you have a God to serve and a soul to save; and if you have anything of religion in you, you will take heed of the thieves of time, and will reserve all opportunities for the best things. How far are they from Christianity who jostle out holy duties! Instead of borrowing time from the world for prayer, they steal time from prayer that they might follow the world.

7. *We make religion our business when we serve God with all our might.* Our strength and spirits are drawn forth about religion. We seek, sweat, strive, and bestir ourselves as in a matter of life and death. We put forth not only diligence but violence. 2 Samuel 6:14: "David danced before the Lord with all his might." This is to make religion our business, when we shake off sloth and put on zeal as a garment. We must not only pray, but pray fervently. We must not only repent, but be "zealous and repent," Revelation 3:19. We must not only love, but be "sick of love," Song of Solomon 2:5. As Horatius wrote,

> *The extremes of heat and cold must often prove,*
> *And shun the weakening joys of wine and love.*

This is to be a Christian with purpose, when we put forth all our vigor and fervor in religion, and take the kingdom of God, as it were, by storm. It is not a faint desire that will bring us to heaven. There must not only be wishing but working; and we must so work as to be damned if we come short.

USE 1. OF INFORMATION.
BRANCH 1. Hence learn that there are but few good Christians. Oh, how few make religion their business! Is he an artificer who never wrought in the trade? Is he a Christian who never wrought in the trade of godliness? How few make religion their business!

Some make religion a complement, but not their business. They court religion by a profession, and, if need be, religion shall have their letters of commendation, but they do not make religion their business. Many of Christ's disciples who said, "Lord, evermore give us this bread," John 6:34, yet soon after basely deserted Christ and would follow Him no more. John 6:66: "From that time, many of His disciples went back and walked no more with Him."

Others make the world their business. "Who mind earthly things," Philippians 3:19. As the earth puts out the fire, so the love of earthly things puts out the fire of heavenly affections. It was a judgment upon Korah and Dathan, Numbers 16:32, "The earth swallowed them up." Thus it is with many; the world swallows up their time, thoughts, and discourse. They are swallowed alive in the earth. There is a lawful use of these things, but the sin is in the excess. The bee may suck a little honey from the leaf, but put it in a barrel of honey and it is drowned. How many engulf themselves in the creature and drive such a trade in the shop that they quite break in their trading for heaven! The farm and oxen have kept millions from Christ. These do not make religion their business, but make the world their business; and what will all be at death but a dream or fancy? Habakkuk 2:13: "The people shall labor in the very fire, and shall weary themselves for very vanity." BRANCH 2. Hence see how hard it is to be saved. It is not as easy as some apprehend. Religion must be our business. It is not enough to have a smack of religion, a touch and sway, but we must make it our business. How many precepts have we to obey, how many temptations to resist, how many graces to treasure up! Religion is the work of our whole lives, and all is little enough! Lord, then how hard is it to be saved! "Where will the sinner appear?" What will become of the gallants of our time who make sin their business, whose whole employment is to indulge and pamper the flesh, lovers of pleasure more than lovers of labor? "All their care is," said Jerome, "to crisp their hair, to sparkle their diamonds; instead of seeping their souls in brinish tears, they bathe themselves in perfumed waters and ride to hell upon the back of pleasure."

USE 2. OF TRIAL.

Let us deal impartially with our own souls, and put ourselves upon a strict trial before the Lord whether we make religion our business or not. And, for our better progress herein, I shall lay down ten signs and characters of a man who makes his religion his business; and by these, as by a gospel touchstone, we may try ourselves.

CHARACTER 1. *He who makes religion his business does not place his religion only in externals.* Romans 2:28: "He is not a Jew who is one outwardly." Religion does not stand only in forms and shadows; this is to give God leaves instead of fruit. It is often seen that the pomp of worship destroys the purity as the paint of the glass hinders the light. And it is no untruth to say that formality may as well damn as profaneness. A superstitious Pharisee may as well be in hell as a drunken epicure. A Christian's main work lies with his heart. He who makes religion his business gives God the vitals; he worships Him in spirit and truth. In distilling, the spirits are strongest. The good Christian distills out the spirits for God. Aaron must offer the fat upon the altar, Leviticus 3:3, 16: "He shall offer an offering made by fire unto the Lord; the fat that covereth the inwards. All the fat is the Lord's." If Aaron had offered the skin instead of the fat, it would not have been accepted. External devotion alone is offering the skin, and they who give God only the skin of religion shall carry away only the shell of comfort.

CHARACTER 2. *He who makes religion his business avoids everything that may be an obstacle or a hindrance to him in his work.* A wicked man does not care whether the matter of religion goes forward or backward. He stands in the way of temptation, and, as if sin did not come fast enough, he draws it as with a cart rope, Isaiah 5:18. But he who makes religion his business flies from temptation; and while he is running the heavenly race he "lays aside every weight of sin which doth so easily beset" him, Hebrews 12:1. A man may as well miss heaven by loitering in the way as by losing. "The king's business required haste," 1 Samuel 21:8, so the business of religion requires haste. Therefore, the good Christian is careful that he is not taken off the work, and so found tardy in it.

CHARACTER 3. *He who makes religion his business has a care to preserve conscience inviolable, and would rather of-*

fend all the world than offend his conscience. 2 Timothy 1:3:
"I thank God, whom I serve from my forefathers with a
pure conscience." Much of religion lies in conscience.
Faith is a precious jewel, but conscience is the cabinet
where this jewel must be kept. 1 Timothy 3:9: "Holding
the mystery of the faith in a pure conscience." 1
Timothy 1:5: "Charity out of a pure heart, and of a
good conscience." So sacred a thing is conscience that
without this all religion drops in pieces. He who makes
religion his business labors to get conscience regulated
by Scripture as the watch is set by the dial, and, having
done this, he keeps his conscience as his eye so that no
dust of sin falls into it.

CHARACTER 4. *He who makes religion his business
sees to it that religion has an influence upon all his civil actions.*

Religion has an influence upon his eating and
drinking. He holds the golden bridle of temperance;
he eats sparingly. As Chrysostom said, "The godly man
feeds not to please the sensual appetite, but that he
may, by the strength he receives from the creature, be
the more fit for the cheerful discharge of spiritual services." He does not make his food fuel for lust, but
help to duty. Epicures dig their own grave with their
teeth; they feed without fear, Jude 12; they are lawless
gluttons. Sinners do not fear lest their table should be
a snare; they do not fear the process of justice. While
the wine is in the cup, they do not fear the handwriting
on the wall. But the godly man, being regulated by religion, puts a knife to his throat that he may cut the
throat of intemperance.

He who makes religion his business sees to it that
religion has an influence upon his recreation. The

strings of the violin must sometimes be slacked lest they break. God affords His people generous delights. The Scripture allows the use of the bow, 2 Samuel 1:18, but we are apt to offend most in lawful things. More are killed with poison. Religion sits as moderator in the soul. The man influenced by religion dares not make play an occupation. It is oil to quicken him in God's service, not a sea to engulf him. He who is devoted to religion puts bounds to the Olympian sports. He knows where to make his stops and periods. He sets up a pillar or boundary as immovable as one of those which bear the name of Hercules, on which he writes, "No further than this!"

He who makes religion his business sees that religion has an influence upon his buying and selling. The wicked get a livelihood often by deception; sometimes they depreciate commodities; they sell the refuse of the wheat, Amos 8:6. They would pick out the best grains of corn and then sell the rest. Sometimes they falsify their weights. Hosea 12:7: "He is a merchant, the balances of deceit are in his hand." But he who makes religion his business is regulated by it in the shop. He is just in his dealings; he dares not hold the Book of God in one hand and false weights in the other. He is faithful to his neighbor, and makes as much reckoning of the Ten Commandments as of his creed.

Religion has an influence upon his marrying. He labors to graft upon a religious stock. He is not so ambitious of parentage as of piety. Nor is his care so much to espouse dowry as virtue. In a word, he seeks for a "helpmeet," one who may help him up the hill to heaven. This is marrying "in the Lord." That marriage indeed is honorable when the husband is joined to one who is the temple of the Holy Ghost. Here is the man who makes religion his business, who, in all his civil transactions, is steered and influenced by religion. Religion is the universal ingredient.

CHARACTER 5. *He who makes religion his business is good in his calling and relations.* Relative grace much graces religion. I shall suspect his goodness who herein is eccentric. Some will pray and discourse well, but it appears they never made religion their business but rather took it up for ostentation than occupation because they are defective in relative duties. They are bad husbands, bad children, etc. If one should draw a picture and leave out an eye, it would greatly eclipse and take from the beauty of the picture. To fail in a relation stains the honor of profession. He who makes religion his business is like a star shining in the proper orb and station wherein God has set him.

CHARACTER 6. *He who makes religion his business has a care of his company.* He dares not twist into a cord of friendship with sinners. Psalm 26:4: "I have not sat with vain persons." Diamonds will not cement with rubbish. It is dangerous to intermingle with the wicked lest their breath prove infectious; sin is very catching. Psalm 106:35-36 says that they "were mingled among the heathen, and learned their works. And they served their idols, which were a snare unto them." If you mingle bright and rusty armor together, the rusty will not be made bright, but the bright will be made rusty. He who makes religion his business does not like to be near those whose nearness sets him further off from God, and whose embraces, like those of the spider, are to suck out the precious life. The godly man engrafts himself into the communion of saints, and hereby, as the scions, he partakes of the sap and virtue of their grace. He who makes it his business to get to heaven associates only with those who may make him better, or whom he may make better.

CHARACTER 7. *He who makes religion his business keeps his spiritual watch always by him.*

He watches his eye. Job 31:1, "I made a covenant with my eyes." When Dinah was gadding, she was defiled, Genesis 34:1-2. When the eye is gadding by impure glances, the heart is defiled.

He who makes religion his business watches his thoughts lest they should turn to froth. Jeremiah 4:14: "How long shall thy vain thoughts lodge within thee?" What a world of sin is minted in the fancy! A child of God sets a spy over his thoughts; he summons them in and takes them captive "to the obedience of Christ," 2 Corinthians 10:5.

He who makes religion his business watches his passions. Passion is like gunpowder, with which the devil, setting on fire, blows up the soul. In a passion, Jonah quarreled with the Almighty, Jonah 4:1, 9. He who is devoted to religion watches his passions lest the tide, growing high, should be carried down the stream and be drowned in it.

He who makes religion his business watches his duties. Matthew 26:41: "Watch and pray."

First, he watches *in* prayer. The heart is subject to remissness; if it is not dead in sin it will be dead in prayer. A Christian watches lest he should abate his fervor in duty. He knows if the strings of his spiritual violin slacken, he cannot "make melody in his heart to the Lord," Ephesians 5:19, Colossians 3:16.

Second, he watches *after* prayer. As a man is most

careful of himself when he comes out of a hot bath, the pores being then most open and subject to cold, so a Christian is most careful when he comes from an ordinance lest his heart should decoy him into sin. Therefore, when he has prayed, he sets a watch. He deals with his heart as the Jews dealt with Christ's sepulcher. Matthew 27:66 says that they "made the sepulcher sure, sealing the stone, and setting a watch." A good Christian, having been at the Word and sacrament (that sealing ordinance), after the sealing sets a watch.

He who makes religion his business watches his temptation. Temptation is the scout which the devil sends out to discover our forces. It is the train he lays to blow up our grace. Satan ever lies at the catch. He has his depths (Revelation 2:24), his methods (Ephesians 4:14), and his devices (2 Corinthians 2:11). He is continually fishing for our souls, and if Satan is angling we need to be watching. He who makes religion his business is full of holy execution. He lies sentinel, and, with the prophet, stands upon his watchtower, Habakkuk 2:1. Solomon said of a virtuous woman, Proverbs 31:18, "Her candle goeth not out by night." The good Christian keeps his watch-candle always burning.

CHARACTER 8. *He who makes religion his business every day casts up his accounts to see how things go in his soul, Lamentations 3:40.* Solomon said, "Know the state of thy flocks," Proverbs 27:23. A man who makes religion his work is careful to know the state of his soul. Before the Lord brings him to a trial, he brings himself to a trial. He would rather use the looking-glass of the Word to see his own heart than put on the broad spectacles of censure to see another's fault. He plays the critic upon himself. He searches what sin is in his heart unrepented of; and, having found it out, he labors by his tears, as by the waters of jealousy, to make the thigh of sin to rot, Numbers 5:22.

He searches whether he has grace or not, and he tries it to see whether it is genuine or spurious. He is as much afraid of painted holiness as he is of going to a painted heaven. He traverses things in his soul and will never leave till that question, whether he is in the faith or not, is put out of question. Here is the man making religion his business. He is loath to be a spiritual bankrupt. Therefore, he is still calling himself to account; and where he comes short he gets Christ to be his Surety.

CHARACTER 9. *He who makes religion his business will be religious whatever it costs him.* He is a resolved man. Psalm 119:106: "I have sworn that I will keep Thy righteous judgments." There are some who will be rich, and there are some who will be godly. He who makes religion his business will not, as Luther said, be put off with other things. He can lack health, riches, or friends, but he cannot lack Christ or grace. He will be godly. Let the times be what they will, they shall not take him off the work of religion. He will follow Christ upon the water; the floods of persecution cannot drown his zeal. He does not say, "There is a lion in the way." He will wrestle with difficulties and march in the face of death. The Christians of the primitive church cried out to the persecutor, "Hew us in pieces, burn us, we will never worship your idols." These were in good earnest for heaven.

There is a great deal of difference between those

who go to sea for pleasure and those mariners who are to go on a voyage to the East Indies. The first, upon the least storm, retreat back to shore; but those who are embarked for a voyage hold onto their course though the sea is rough and stormy, and will venture their lives in hope of the golden harvest at the Indies. Hypocrites seem religious when things are serene and calm, but they will not sail in a storm. Only those who make religion their business will hold out their voyage to heaven in the midst of tempests and death-threatening dangers.

CHARACTER 10. *He who makes religion his business lives every day as his last day.* He prays in the morning as if he were to die at night. He lives as if he were presently to be called to God's bar. He walks "soberly, righteously, and godly," Titus 2:12. He girds his loins, trims his lamp, and sets his house in order that when death comes for him with a *habeas corpus* he may have nothing to do but die. Behold here the man who makes religion his business.

USE 3. OF EXHORTATION.

Let me persuade all you whose consciences may smite you for former neglects—now set upon the work; make religion your business; bestir yourselves in this as in a matter of life and death.

QUESTION. But what must we do to make religion our business?

ANSWER. That you may be serious in this work, I shall lay down several rules for your help and direction therein.

Rules for Making Religion Our Business

RULE 1. *If you would make religion your business, possess yourselves with this maxim, that religion is the end of your creation.* God never sent men into the world only to eat and drink and put on fine clothes, but the end of their creation is to honor Him. 1 Peter 4:11: "That God in all things may be glorified." Should the body only be tended and looked after, this would be to trim the scabbard instead of the blade. It would be to invert and frustrate the very end of our being.

RULE 2. *If you would make religion your business, get a change of heart wrought.* Breathe after a principle of holiness. He cannot make religion his business who has no religion. Can the body move without a principle of life? Christian, get your heart spiritualized by grace. An earthly heart will no more trade in heaven than a millstone will ascend or a serpent fly in the air. The heart must be divinely touched with the Spirit, like a needle with the magnet, before it can cleave to God and follow Him fully, Numbers 14:24. Never expect the practice to be holy till there is first a holy principle.

RULE 3. *If you would make religion your business, set yourselves always under the eye of God.* The master's eye makes the servant work. God's eye will quicken our devotion. Psalm 16:8: "I have set the Lord always before me." If we leave off work, or loiter in our work, God sees. He has a window which opens into our breasts. This is, as Chrysostom called it, "the eye of God that never sleeps," and would make us active in the sphere of duty. If, indeed, God's eye were at any time off of us, we might slacken our pace in religion. But He is ever looking on. If we take the wings of the morning we

cannot fly from His presence. And He who is now the
Spectator will be the Judge. Oh, how would this con-
sideration of God's omniscience keep us from being
truants in religion! How would it infuse a spirit of activity and gallantry into us, making us put forward with all
our might in the race to heaven!

RULE 4. *If you would make religion your business, think
often of the shortness of time.* This life is but a vapor, James
4:14; a shadow, 1 Chronicles 29:5; it is as nothing,
Psalm 39:5. We are wheeling apace out of the world,
and there is no work to be done for our souls in the
grave. Ecclesiastes 9:10: "Whatsoever thy hand findeth
to do, do it with thy might; for there is no work, nor
device, in the grave, whither thou goest." Now is the
time of life; now is the day of grace. You do not know
how soon these two suns may set. The shorter our life,
the swifter should be our pace.

RULE 5. *If you would make religion your business, get
an understanding heart.* Weigh things seriously in the
balance of reason and judgment. Think of the infinite
importance of this business—our eternal misery or
happiness depends upon it. Other things are but for
convenience; this is of necessity. If this work is not
done, we are undone. If we do not do the work which
believers are doing, we must do the work which devils
are doing. And if God gives us a serious heart to lay
ourselves out in the business of religion, our income
will be greater than our expense. Religion is a good
trade if it is well followed. It will remit the cost; it is like
working in silver. 1 Peter 1:9: "Receiving the end of
your faith, even the salvation of your souls." God will
shortly take us from the working house to the throne,
and will set upon our head a fresh garland made of the

flowers of paradise.
RULE 6. *If you would make religion your business, implore the help of God's Spirit.* All we can do is but lost labor unless the Spirit excites and accelerates. Beg a gale from heaven. Song of Solomon 4:16: "Awake, O north wind, and come thou south; blow upon my garden." If the Spirit joins with our chariot, then we move to heaven swiftly like a roe upon the mountains or as the chariots of Amminadib, Song of Solomon 2:17, 6:12.

Now, having laid down the rules, let me, for a conclusion, press all Christians to this great duty of making religion their business. And I will use but two weighty considerations.

1. The sweetness that is in religion. All her paths are pleasantness, Proverbs 3:17. The way of religion is strewn with roses in regard to that inward peace which God gives. Psalm 19:11: "In keeping Thy precepts there is great reward." As while the mother tends her child, and sometimes beyond her strength too, yet finds a secret delight in it; so, while a Christian is serving God, there is that inward contentment and delight infused; and he meets with such transfigurations of soul that he thinks himself half in heaven. It was Christ's meat and drink to do His Father's will, John 4:34. Religion was Paul's recreation, Romans 7:22. Though I should not speak of wages, the joys which God gives us in this life are enough to make us be in love with His service.

2. Millions of persons have miscarried to eternity for want of making religion their business. They have done something in religion, but not to any purpose. They have begun, but have made too many stops and pauses. They have been lukewarm and neutral in the

business. They have served God as if they served Him
not. They have sinned fervently but prayed faintly.
Religion has been a thing only by the by. They have
served God by fits and starts, but have not made
religion their business. Therefore, they have
miscarried to all eternity.

If you could see a wicked man's tombstone in hell,
you might read this inscription upon it: "Here lies one
in hellish flames for not making religion his business."
How many ships have suffered shipwreck, notwithstanding all their glorious names of "The Hope," "The
Safeguard," and "The Triumph"! So how many souls,
notwithstanding their glorious title of saintship, have
suffered shipwreck in hell forever because they have
not made religion their business!

The Day of Judgment Asserted

"Because He hath appointed a day, in the which He will judge the world in righteousness by that man whom He hath ordained; whereof he hath given assurance unto all men, in that He hath raised Him from the dead." Acts 17:31

When St. Paul perceived the idolatry at Athens, "his spirit was stirred in him," verse 16. His spirit was soured and embittered in him. Paul was a bitter man against sin; that anger is without sin which is against sin. Or, the word may signify, he was in a paroxysm, or burning fit of zeal. And zeal is such a passion as cannot be either dissembled or pent up; with this fire he discharged against their idolatry. "Ye men of Athens, I perceive that in all things ye are too superstitious. For as I passed by, and beheld your devotions, I found an altar with this description, 'To the Unknown God,' " verses 22-23. Nor does the Apostle only declaim against the false god, but declare to them the true God. And he does it from the effect: "That God who made the world and all things therein . . . is Lord of heaven and earth," verse 24. To create is the best demonstration of a Deity. And this God, being everywhere by way of repletion, cannot be locally confined. Acts 17:24: "He dwelleth not in temples made with hands." And though in former times, when the veil of ignorance was drawn over the face of the world, God seemed less severe—"The times of this ignorance God winked at"—though He did, as it were, "overlook" them, not taking the extremity of the law, yet "now He commandeth all men everywhere to repent," verse 30. And if it is asked, "Why *now* repent? Why may we not take our full sleep?" the reason is because *now* is the broad daylight of the gospel, which, as it reveals sin more clearly, so it more clearly reveals judgment upon sinners: "He hath appointed a day in which He will judge the world."

These words are God's alarm to the world to awaken it out of security. This is a sweet yet dreadful point. When St. Paul discoursed of judgment to come, Felix trembled, Acts 24:25. He who is not affected with this truth has a heart of stone.

For the illustration of this, there are six things I shall discuss:
1. There shall be a day of judgment.
2. Why there must be a day of judgment.
3. When the day of judgment shall be.
4. Who shall be the Judge.
5. The order and the method of the trial.
6. The effect or consequence of it.

1. I begin with the first: *There shall be a day of judgment.* There is a twofold day of judgment:
(1) A particular judgment. At the day of death, immediately upon the soul's dissolution from the body, it has a judgment passed upon it, Hebrews 9:27. "Then shall the dust return to the earth as it was: and the spirit shall return unto God that gave it," Ecclesiastes 12:7. As soon as the breath expires, the soul receives its

particular sentence and knows how it shall be with it to all eternity.

(2) There is a general day of judgment, which is the great judgment, when the world shall be gathered together. And of this the text is to be understood: "He hath appointed a day in the which He will judge the world." I might give you a whole jury of Scriptures giving their verdict to this, but in the mouth of two or three witnesses the truth will be confirmed. "God shall bring every work into judgment, with every secret thing, whether it be good, or whether it be evil," Ecclesiastes 12:14. "Every idle word that men shall speak, they shall give account thereof in the day of judgment," Matthew 12:36. *Now* is the day of arrears; *then* will be the day of account. "For He cometh, for He cometh to judge the earth," Psalm 96:13. The repetition denotes the certainty and infallibility of His coming.

2. *Why there must be a day of judgment.*

(1) That God may execute justice on the wicked. Things seem to be carried here in the world with an unequal balance. The "candle of God shines upon" the wicked, Job 29:3. "They that tempt God are even delivered," Malachi 3:15. Diogenes, seeing Harpalus, a thief, go on prosperously, said that surely God had cast off the government of the world, and did not mind how things went here below. "There shall come in the last days scoffers, saying, Where is the promise of His coming?" 2 Peter 3:3-4. Therefore, God will have a day of judgment to vindicate His justice. He will let sinners know that long forbearance is no forgiveness.

(2) That God may exercise mercy to the godly.

Here piety was the white which was shot at. They who prayed and wept had the hardest measure. Those Christians whose zeal flamed most met with the fiery trial. "For Thy sake we are killed all the day long; we are accounted as sheep for the slaughter," Romans 8:36. "The saints," said Cyprian, "are put in the wine-press, and oft the blood of these grapes is pressed out." God will therefore have a day of judgment that He may reward all the tears and sufferings of His people. They shall have their crown and throne and white robes, Revelation 7:9; though they may be losers *for* Him, they shall lose nothing *by* Him.

3. *When the day of judgment shall be.*
    It is certain there shall be a judgment; it is uncertain when. The angels do not know the day, nor does Christ either as He was man (Matthew 24:36; Mark 13:32). And the reason why the time is not known is:
    (1) That we may not be curious. There are some things which God would have us be ignorant of. "It is not for you to know the times or the seasons, which the Father hath put in His own power," Acts 1:7. We must not pry into God's ark or meddle with his secrets of government. As Salvian said, "It is a kind of sacrilege for any man to break into the Holy of Holies and enter into God's secrets."
    (2) God has concealed the time of judgment that we may not be careless. We are always to keep sentinel, having our loins girded and our lamps burning, not knowing how soon that day may overtake us. Austin said, "God would have us live every day as if the last day were approaching."

Believe that every morning's ray
Hath lighted up thy latest day.

This is the genuine use which our Savior makes of it. Mark 13:32-33: "Of that day and hour knoweth no man, no, not the angels which are in heaven. Take ye heed, watch and pray: for ye know not when the time is."

But though we cannot know precisely when this day of the Lord shall be, yet in probability the time cannot be far off. Hebrews 10:37: "He that shall come will come, and will not tarry." Chrysostom had a simile: "When we see an old man going on crutches, his joints weak, his radical moisture dried up; though we do not know the just time when he will die, yet it is sure he cannot live long because nature's stock is spent. So the world is decrepit and goes, as it were, upon crutches. Therefore it cannot be long before the world's funerals, and the birthday of judgment."

The age which St. John wrote in was "the last time," 1 John 2:18. In the Greek it is "the last hour." Then surely the time we now live in may be called "the last minute." Psalm 96:13: "For He cometh to judge the earth." It is not "He shall come," but "He cometh," to show how near the time is. It is almost daybreak and the court is ready to sit. James 5:9: "The Judge standeth at the door."

Verily, if security, apostasy, decay of love, inundation of sin, and revelation of Antichrist are made in Scripture the symptoms and prognostications of the last day, we, having these gray hairs among us, know that the day of judgment cannot be far off.

4. *Who shall be the Judge?*

I answer, the Lord Jesus Christ. Thus it is in the text: "He will judge the world by that man whom He hath ordained," that man who is God-man. We must take heed of judging others; this is Christ's work. John 5:22: "The Father hath committed all judgment unto the Son." He who once had a reed put into His hand, His Father will now put a scepter into His hand. He who had a purple robe put upon Him in derision shall come in His Judge's robes. He who hung upon the cross shall sit upon the bench. There are two things in Christ which eminently qualify Him to be a Judge:

(1) Prudence and intelligence to understand all causes that are brought before Him. He is described with seven eyes in Zechariah 3:9, to note His omniscience. He is like Ezekiel's wheels, full of eyes, Ezekiel 10:12. Christ is a heart-searcher. He not only judges the fact but the heart, which no angel can do.

(2) Strength whereby He is able to be avenged upon His enemies. Christ is armed with sovereignty; therefore the seven stones are said to be upon one stone, Zechariah 3:9, to denote the infinite strength of Christ. And He is described with seven horns, Revelation 5:6. As Christ has an eye to see, so He has a horn to push; as He has His balance, so He has His sword; as He has His fan and His sieve, so He has His lake of fire, Revelation 20:10.

5. *The order and method of the trial.*

Observe: (1) the summons; (2) the Judge's coming to the bench; and (3) the process and trial itself.

(1) The summons to the court, and that is by the sounding of the trumpet. 1 Thessalonians 4:16: "The

Lord Himself shall descend from heaven with a shout, with the voice of the archangel, and with the trump of God." St. Jerome said that whatever he was doing he thought he heard the noise of the trumpet sounding in his ears. "Arise, ye dead, and come to judgment." Note:

The shrillness of the trumpet. It shall sound so loud that the dead shall hear it.

The efficacy of the trumpet. It shall not only startle the dead, but raise them out of their graves, Matthew 24:31. They who will not hear the trumpet of the ministry sounding but lie dead in sin shall be sure to hear the trumpet of the archangel sounding.

(2) The manner of the Judge's coming to the bench. Christ's coming to judgment will be glorious yet dreadful.

It will be glorious to the godly. The Apostle calls it, Titus 2:13: "the glorious appearing of the great God and our Savior Jesus Christ."

Christ's person shall be glorious. At His first coming in the flesh His glory was veiled over, Isaiah 53:2-3; all who saw the man did not see the Messiah. But His second coming will be very illustrious and resplendent. He shall "come in the glory of His Father," Mark 8:38. That is, He shall wear the same embroidered robes of majesty as His Father.

Christ's attendants shall be glorious. He "shall come with all His holy angels," Matthew 25:31. These sublime, seraphic spirits, who for their luster are compared to lightning, Matthew 28:3, are Christ's satellites, part of Christ's train and retinue. He who was led to the cross with a band of soldiers shall be attended to the bench with a guard of angels.

Christ's coming to judgment will be dreadful to the

wicked. At the coming of this Judge, there will be a fire
burning round about Him. He "shall be revealed from
heaven with His mighty angels, in flaming fire, taking
vengeance on them that know not God, and that obey
not the gospel of our Lord Jesus Christ," 2 Thessalonians 1:7-8. When God gave His law upon the mount,
"there were thunders and lightnings; and Mount Sinai
was altogether on a smoke, because the Lord descended upon it in fire," Exodus 19:16-18. "If God was
so terrible at the giving of the law, O how terrible will
He be when He shall come to require His law?" said
Augustine.

(3) The process or the trial itself, where observe the
universality, the formality, and the circumstances of
the trial.

The universality of the trial. It will be a very great assize; never was the like seen. "For we must all appear
before the judgment seat of Christ," 2 Corinthians
5:10. Kings and nobles, councils and armies, those who
were above all trial here, have no charter of exemption
granted them. They must appear before Christ's tri-
bunal and be tried for their lives. Neither power nor
policy can be a subterfuge. They who refused to come
to the throne of grace shall be forced to come to the
bar of justice. And the dead as well as the living must
make their appearance. Revelation 20:12: "I saw the
dead, both small and great, stand before God." We do
not usually cite men in our courts when they are dead,
but at that day the dead are called to the bar; and not
only men but angels. Jude 6: "The angels which kept
not their first estate, but left their own habitation, He
hath reserved in everlasting chains under darkness
unto the judgment of the great day."

The formality of the trial, which consists in the opening of the books. Daniel 7:10 and Revelation 20:12: "The judgment was set, and the books were opened." There are two books that will be opened:

First, the book of God's omniscience. God not only observes, but registers all our actions. Job 14:16: "Thou numberest my steps." The word there "to number" signifies to put a thing into a book. It is as if Job had said, "Lord, Thou keepest Thy daybook and enterest down all my actions into the book." We read of God's book of remembrance, Malachi 3:16. This book will be produced at the last day.

Second, the book of conscience. Let there never be so much written in a book, yet, if it is clasped, it is not seen. Men have their sins written in their conscience, but the book is clasped (the searing of the conscience is the clasping of the book); but when this book of conscience shall be unclasped at the great day, then all their hypocrisy, treason, and atheism shall appear to the view of men and angels, Luke 12:3. The sins of men shall be written upon their forehead as with a pen of iron.

The circumstances of the trial. Where consider four things: the impartiality, the exactness, the perspicuity, and the supremacy.

• The impartiality of the trial. Jesus Christ will do every man justice. He will, as the text says, "judge the world in righteousness." It will be a day of equitable judgment; justice holds the scales. The Thebans pictured their judges as being blind and without hands—blind, that they might not respect persons, and without hands, that they might take no bribes. Christ's scepter is a scepter of righteousness, Hebrews 1:8. He is no respecter of persons, Acts 10:34. It is not nearness of blood that prevails; many of Christ's kindred shall be condemned. It is not gloriousness of profession; many shall go to hell with Christ in their mouths. Matthew 7:22: "Many will say to Me in that day, Lord, Lord, have we not prophesied in Thy name? And in Thy name cast out devils? And in Thy name done many wonderful works?" Yet, though they cast out devils, they are cast out to the devil. It is not the varnish of a picture that a judicious eye is taken with, but the curiousness of the work. It is not the most shining profession which Christ is taken with, unless he sees the curious workmanship of grace in the heart drawn by the pencil of the Holy Ghost. Things are not carried there by parties "but in a most just balance." Christ has true weights for false hearts. There are no fees taken in that court. The judge will not be bribed with a hypocritical tear or a Judas kiss.

• The exactness of the trial. It will be very critical. Then will Christ thoroughly purge His floor, Matthew 3:12. Not a grace or a sin but His fan will discover. Christ will, at the day of judgment, make a heart anatomy, as the surgeon makes a dissection in the body and evaluates several body parts, or as the goldsmith brings his gold to the balance and touchstone and pierces his gold through to see if it is right and genuine, and whether there is not a baser metal within. Thus the Lord Jesus, whose eyes are as a flame of fire, Revelation 1:14, will pierce through the hearts of men and see if there is the right metal within, having the image and superscription of God upon it. Paint falls off in the fire. The hypocrite's paint will fall off at the fiery trial. Nothing then will stand us in stead but sincerity.

• The perspicuity of the trial. Sinners shall be so clearly convicted that they shall hold up their hand at the bar and cry, "Guilty." Those words of David may be fitly applied here: "That Thou mightest be clear when Thou judgest," Psalm 51:4. The sinner himself shall clear God of injustice. The Greek word for vengeance signifies "justice." God's taking vengeance is doing justice. Sin makes God angry, but it cannot make Him unrighteous. The wicked shall drink a sea of wrath, but not sip one drop of injustice. Christ will say, "Sinner, what apology can you make for yourself? Are not your sins written in the book of conscience? Did you not have that book in your own keeping? Who could have inserted anything into it?" Now the sinner, being self-condemned, shall clear his Judge: "Lord, though I am damned, yet I have no wrong done me. Thou art clear when Thou judgest."

• The supremacy of the court. This is the highest court of judicature, from whence is no appeal. Men can remove their causes from one place to another, from the Common Law to the Court of Chancery, but from Christ's court there is no appeal. He who is once doomed here finds his condition irreversible.

6. *The sixth and last particular is the effect or consequence of the trial, which consists in three things:*

(1) Segregation. Christ will separate the godly and the wicked. Matthew 25:32: "He shall separate them from one another, as a shepherd divideth his sheep from the goats." Then will be the great day of separation. It is a great grief to the godly in this life that they live among the wicked. Psalm 120:5: "Woe is me, that I sojourn in Meshech, that I dwell in the tents of Kedar."

Wicked men blaspheme God, Psalm 74:18, and persecute the saints, 2 Timothy 3:12. They are compared to
dogs, Psalm 22:16; to bulls, Psalm 68:30; and to lions,
Psalm 57:4. They roar upon the godly and tear them as
their prey. Cain kills, Ishmael mocks, Shimei rails. The
godly and the wicked are now promiscuously mingled
together, Matthew 13:30, and this is as offensive as ty-
ing a dead man to a living. But Christ will ere long
make a separation, as the fan separates the wheat from
the chaff, as a furnace separates the gold from the
dross, or as a fine sieve strains the spirit from the dregs.
Christ will put the sheep by themselves who have the
earmark of election upon them, and the goats by
themselves, after which separation there follows:

(2) The sentence, which is twofold:

First, the sentence of absolution pronounced upon
the godly. "Come, ye blessed of My Father, inherit the
kingdom prepared for you from the foundation of the
world," Matthew 25:34. After the pronouncing of this
blessed sentence, the godly shall go from the bar and
sit on the bench with Christ. 1 Corinthians 6:2: "Know
ye not that the saints shall judge the world?" The saints
shall be with Christ's assessors; they shall sit with Him
in judicature as the justices of peace sit with the judge.
They shall vote with Christ and applaud Him in all His
judicial proceedings. Here the world judges the saints,
but there the saints shall judge the world.

Second, the sentence of condemnation pronounced upon the wicked. "Depart from Me, ye
cursed, into everlasting fire, prepared for the devil and
his angels," Matthew 25:41. I may allude to James 3:10:
"Out of the same mouth proceedeth blessing and cursing." Out of the same mouth of Christ proceeds bless-

ing to the godly and cursing to the wicked." The same wind which brings one ship to the haven blows another ship upon the rock. "Depart from Me." The wicked once said to God, "Depart." Job 21:14: "They say unto God, Depart from us." And now God will say to them, "Depart from Me." This will be a heart-rending word. Chrysostom said, "This word 'depart!' is worse than the fire." Psalm 16:11: "Depart from Me, in whose presence is fullness of joy."

Third, after this sentence follows the execution. Matthew 13:30: "Bind the tares in bundles to burn them." Christ will say, "Bundle up these sinners. Here are a bundle of hypocrites, there a bundle of apostates, there a bundle of profane persons. Bind them up and throw them in the fire." And no cries or entreaties will prevail with the Judge. The sinner and the fire must keep one another company. He who would not weep for his sins must burn for them.

It is "everlasting fire." The three children were thrown into the fire, but they did not stay in long. Daniel 3:26: "Nebuchadnezzar came near to the mouth of the burning fiery furnace, and spake, and said, Shadrach, Meshach, and Abednego, ye servants of the most high God, come forth, and come hither. Then Shadrach, Meshach, and Abednego came forth of the midst of the fire." But the fire of the damned is everlasting fire. This word "ever" breaks the heart. Length of time cannot terminate it; a sea of tears cannot quench it. The wrath of God is the fire and the breath of God the bellows to blow it up to all eternity. Oh, how dreadfully tormenting will this fire be! To endure it will be intolerable; to avoid it will be impossible.

USE 1. OF PERSUASION.

Let me persuade all Christians to believe this truth that there shall be a day of judgment. "Rejoice, O young man, in thy youth; and let thy heart cheer thee in the days of thy youth, and walk in the ways of thine heart, and in the sight of thine eyes: but know thou, that for all these things God will bring thee into judgment," Ecclesiastes 11:9. This is a great article of our faith, that Christ shall come to judge the quick and the dead. Yet how many live as if this article were blotted out of their creed! We have too many epicures and atheists who drown themselves in sensual delights and live as if they did not believe either in God or the day of judgment. The Lucianists and Platonists deny the immortality of the soul; the Photinians hold there is no hell. I have read of the Duke of Silesia who was so infatuated that he did not believe either God or the devil. I wish there were not too many of this duke's opinion. Would men dare swear, be unchaste, or live in malice if they believed in a day of judgment? Oh, mingle this text with faith. "The Lord hath appointed a day in which He will judge the world." There must be such a day. Not only does Scripture assert it, but reason confirms it. There is no kingdom or nation in the world but has its sessions and courts of judicature; and shall not God, who sets up all other courts, be allowed His? That there shall be a day of judgment is engrafted by nature in the consciences of men. Peter Martyr tells us that some of the heathen poets have written that there are certain judges appointed (Minos, Rhadamanthus, and others) to examine and punish offenders after this life.

USE 2. OF INFORMATION.

See here the sad and deplorable estate of wicked men. This text is as the handwriting on the wall which may make their "knees to smite one against another," Daniel 5:6. The wicked shall come to judgment, but they "shall not stand in the judgment," Psalm 1:5. In the Hebrew it is "they shall not rise up." God shall be decked with glory and majesty, His face as the appearance of lightning, His eyes as lamps of fire, and a sword of justice in His hand, and shall call the sinner by name and say, "Stand forth. Answer to the charge that is brought against you. What can you say for your pride, oaths, drunkenness? These sins you have been told of by My ministers whom I sent rising up early and going to bed late; but you persisted in your wickedness with a neck of iron, a brow of brass, and a heart of stone. All the tools which I wrought with were broken and worn out upon your rocky spirit. What can you say for yourself that the sentence should not be passed?"

Oh, how amazed and confused will the sinner be! He will be found speechless; he will not be able to look his Judge in the face. Job 31:14: "What then shall I do when God riseth up? And when He visiteth, what shall I answer Him?" Oh, wretch, you who can now outface your minister and your godly parents, when they tell you of sin—you shall not be able to outface your Judge. When God rises up, the sinner's countenance will be fallen.

Not many years ago, the bishops used to visit in their diocese, and call several persons before them as criminal. All the world is God's diocese, and shortly He is coming on His visitation and will call men to account. Now, when God shall visit, how shall the impure

soul be able to answer Him? 1 Peter 4:18: "Where shall
the ungodly and the sinner appear?" You who die in
your sin are sure to be cast at the bar. John 3:18: "He
that believeth not is condemned already." That is, he is
as sure to be condemned as if he were condemned already. And once the sentence of damnation is passed,
miserable man, what will you do? Where will you go?
Will you seek help from God? He is a consuming fire.
Will you seek help from the world? It will be all on fire
about you. From the saints? Those you derided on
earth. From the good angels? They defy you as God's
enemy. From the bad angels? They are your execu-
tioners. From your conscience? There is the worm that
gnaws. From mercy? The lease is run out. Oh, the horror and hellish despair which will seize upon sinners at
that day! Oh, the sad convulsions! Their heads shall
hang down, their cheeks blush, their lips quiver, their
hands shake, their conscience roar, and their heart
tremble. What stupefying medicine has the devil given
to men that they are insensible of the danger they are
in? The cares of the world have so filled their head,
and the profits of it have so bewitched their heart, that
they mind neither death nor judgment.

USE 3. OF EXHORTATION.
BRANCH 1. Possess yourselves with the thoughts of
the day of judgment. Think of the solemnity and impartiality of this court. Feathers swim upon the water;
gold sinks into it. Light, feathery spirits float in vanity,
but serious Christians sink deep in the thoughts of
judgment. Many people are like quicksilver; they cannot be made to fix. If the ship is not well ballasted, it
will soon overturn. The reason why so many are over-

turned with the vanities of the world is that they are
not well ballasted with the thoughts of the day of judgment. Were a man to be tried for his life, he would
think to himself of all the arguments he could to plead
in his own defense. We are all shortly to be tried for
our souls. While others are thinking how they may
grow rich, let us think to ourselves how we may abide
the day of Christ's coming. The serious thoughts of
judgment would be:

First, a curbing bit to sin. "Am I stealing the forbid-
den fruit and the judgment so near?"

Second, a spur to holiness. 2 Peter 3:10-11: "But the
day of the Lord will come as a thief in the night; in the
which the heavens shall pass away with a great noise,
and the elements shall melt with fervent heat, the
earth also and the works that are therein shall be
burned up. Seeing then that all these things shall be
dissolved, what manner of persons ought ye to be in all
holy conversation and godliness?"

BRANCH 2. Let us solemnly prepare ourselves for
this last and great trial. That is, by setting up a judgment seat in our own souls, let us begin a private session before the assizes. It is wisdom to bring our souls
first to trial. Lamentations 3:40: "Let us search and try
our ways." Let us judge ourselves according to the rule
of the Word and let conscience bring in the verdict.
The Word of God gives several characters of a man
who shall be absolved at the day of judgment and is
sure to go to heaven:

Character 1. The first character is humility. Job
22:29: "The Lord shall save the humble person." Now,
let conscience bring in the verdict. Christian, are you
humble? Not only humbled, but humble? Do you es-

teem others better than thyself? Philippians 2:3. Do
you cover your duties with the veil of humility, as
Moses put a veil on his face when it shone? If conscience brings in this verdict, you are sure to be acquit-
ted at the last day.

Character 2. Love to the saints. 1 John 3:14: "We
know that we have passed from death unto life, because we love the brethren." Love makes us like God; it
is the root of all the graces. Does conscience witness
this for you? Are you perfumed with this sweet spice of
love? Do you delight in those who have the image of
God? Do you reverence their graces? Do you bear with
their infirmities? Do you love to see Christ's picture in
a saint, though hung in never so poor a frame? This is
a good sign that you shall pass for currency at the day
of judgment.

Character 3. A penitential frame of heart. Acts 11:18:
"Repentance unto life." Repentance unravels sin and
makes it not to be. Jeremiah 50:20: "In those days the
iniquity of Israel shall be sought for, and there shall be
none." A great ball of snow is melted and washed away
with the rain; great sins are washed away by holy tears.
Now, can conscience bring in the evidence for you? Do
you tune the penitential string? Ambrose asked, "You
who have sinned with Peter, do you weep with Peter?"
And do your tears drop from the eye of faith? This is a
blessed sign that you are judgment-proof, and that
when your iniquities shall be sought at the last day they
shall not be found.

Character 4. Equity in our dealings. "Who shall ascend into the hill of the Lord? Or who shall stand in
His holy place?" Psalm 24:3-4. "He that hath clean
hands." Injustice sullies and defiles the hand. What

does conscience say? Is your hand clean? It is a vain thing to hold the Bible in one hand and false weights in the other.

Beloved, if conscience, upon a Scripture trial, gives in the verdict for us, it is a blessed sign that we shall lift up our heads with boldness at the last day. Conscience is God's echo in the soul. The voice of conscience is the voice of God, and if conscience, upon an impartial trial, acquits us, God will acquit us. 1 John 3:21: "If our heart condemns us not, then have we confidence toward God." If we are absolved in the lower court of conscience, we are sure to be absolved at the last day in the high court of justice. It would be a sweet thing for a Christian thus to bring himself to a trial. Seneca tells us of a Roman who every day called himself to account: "What infirmity is healed? How have you grown better?" Then he would lie down at night with these words: "Oh, how sweet and refreshing is my sleep to me!"

USE 4. OF CONSOLATION.

Here is a fountain of consolation opened to a believer, and that in three cases: 1. Discouraging fear; 2. Weakness of grace; and 3. Censures of the world.

Case 1. Here is comfort in case of discouraging fear. "Oh," said a believer, "I fear my grace is not invincible armor. I fear the cause will go against me at the last day." Indeed, so it would if you were out of Christ. But, as in our law courts the client has his attorney or advocate to plead for him, so every believer, by virtue of the interest he has in Christ, has Christ to plead his cause for him. 1 John 2:1: "If any man sin, we have an Advocate with the Father, Jesus Christ the righteous."

What if Satan is the accuser if Christ is the Advocate?
Christ never lost any cause that He pleaded. Nay, His
very pleading alters the nature of the cause. Christ will
show the debt book crossed with His own blood. And it
is no matter what is charged if all is discharged. Here is
a believer's comfort—his Judge will be his Advocate.

Case 2. Here is comfort with regard to weakness of
grace. A Christian, seeing his grace is so defective, is
ready to be discouraged. But at the day of judgment, if
Christ finds but a small coin of sincerity, it shall be accepted. If yours is true gold, though it may be light,
Christ will put His merits into the scales and make it
sufficient. He who has no sin of allowance shall have
grains of allowance. I may allude to that verse in Amos
9:9, "Yet shall not the least grain fall to the earth." He
who has but a grain of grace, not the least grain shall
fall to hell.

Case 3. It is comfort in case of censures and slan-
ders. The saints go here through strange reports,
"through evil report and a good report," 2 Corinthians
6:8. John the Baptist's head on a platter is a common
dish nowadays. It is ordinary to bring in a saint be-
headed of his good name. But at the day of judgment
Christ will unload His people of all their injuries. He
will vindicate them from all their calumnies. Christ will
be the saint's character witness. He, at that day, will
present His Church "not having spot or wrinkle,"
Ephesians 5:27.

How God Is His People's Great Reward

"I am thy shield, and thy exceeding great reward." Genesis 15:1

Abraham is called "the friend of God," James 2:23. The Lord spoke with him familiarly, Genesis 17:22; he was made of God's privy council, Genesis 18:17. And in the text, "the Word of the Lord came unto him in a vision." Representations of things in a vision differ from revelations by dreams, Genesis 31:11. And what was the word that came to this holy patriarch in a vision? "I am thy shield, and thy exceeding great reward"—words too great for any man or angel fully to expound. Both the Hebrew and Greek carry the phrase very high: "I am thy superabundant, very exceeding much reward." In the text is a climax; it rises like the waters of the sanctuary, higher: I am *thy* reward; thy *great* reward; and thy *exceeding* great reward. There are four things here to be spoken of:

1. Nothing besides God can be the saints' reward.
2. How God is their reward.
3. How God comes to be their reward.
4. Wherein the exceeding greatness of this reward consists.

1. *Nothing besides God can be the saints' reward.*

Nothing on earth can be their reward. The glittering of the world dazzles men's eyes; but, like the apples of Sodom, it does not so much delight as delude. The world is gilded emptiness. The world is made circular; the heart in the figure of a triangle. A circle cannot fill a triangle. The world is enough to busy us, not to fill us. Job 20:22: "In the fullness of his sufficiency he shall be in straits." It seems a riddle to have sufficiency, yet not have enough. The meaning is, when he enjoys most of the creature, yet there is something lacking. When King Solomon had put all the creatures into a cup, and went to extract and distill out the spirits, they turned to froth. "All is vanity," Ecclesiastes 1:2. God never intended that we should dig happiness out of the earth which He has cursed.

Heaven itself is not a saint's reward. Psalm 73:25: "Whom have I in heaven but Thee?" Musculus said, "There are angels and archangels." Aye, but though these are for a saint's comfort, yet not properly for his reward. Communion with seraphims is excellent, yet can no more make a saint's reward than the light of the stars can make day.

2. *How is God His people's reward?*

In bestowing Himself upon them. The great blessing of the covenant is, "I am thy God." The Lord told Abraham that kings should come out of his loins, and He would give the land of Canaan to him and his seed, Genesis 17:6. But all this did not amount to blessedness. That which made up the portion was, "I will be their God," verse 8. God will not only see that the saints shall be rewarded, but He Himself will be their reward. A king may reward his subjects with gratuities, but he bestows himself upon his queen. God said to every believer, as He did to Aaron, "I am thy part and thine inheritance," Numbers 18:20, and as the king of Israel said to Benhadad, "I am thine, and all that I have," 1 Kings 20:4.

Abraham sent away the sons of the concubines with a few gifts, but he settled the inheritance upon Isaac, Genesis 25:5-6. God sent away the wicked with riches and honor, but made Himself over to His people. They have not only the gift but the Giver. And what more can be said? As Micah said, "What have I more?" Judges 18:24. So what has God more to give than Himself? What greater dowry is there than the Deity? God is not only the saints' rewarder, but He is their reward. Job 22:25: "The Almighty shall be thy gold," for so does the Hebrew word import. The sum of all is this: The saints' portion lies in God. Psalm 16:5: "The Lord is the portion of mine inheritance and of my cup."

QUESTION. But how does God give Himself to His people? Is not His essence incommunicable?

ANSWER. True, the saints cannot partake of God's very essence (an error of Montanus and the Familists); the riches of the Deity are too great to be received in specie. But the saints shall have all in God that may be for their comfort. They shall partake so much of God's likeness, His love, His influence, and the irradiations of His glory (1 John 3:2; John 17:26) as astonishes and fills the vessels of mercy, that they run over with joy.

3. *How God comes to be His people's reward.*

Through Jesus Christ—His blood, being the blood of God, has merited this glorious reward for them, Acts

20:28. Though in respect of free grace this reward is a donation, yet in respect of Christ's blood it is a purchase, Ephesians 1:14. How precious should Christ be to us! Had not He died, the portion would never have come into our hands.

4. *Wherein the exceeding greatness of this reward consists.*
God is a satisfying reward. Genesis 17:1: "I am God Almighty." The word for Almighty signifies "Him who has sufficiency." God is a whole ocean of blessedness, so that the soul, while it is bathing in it, cries out in a divine ecstasy, "I have enough." Here is fullness, but no excess. Psalm 17:15: "I shall be satisfied when I awake with Thy likeness." When I awake out of the sleep of death, having my soul embellished with the illustrious beams of Thy glory, I shall be satisfied. In God there is not only sufficiency but redundancy; not only the fullness of the vessel, but the fullness of the fountain. When the whole world was defaced, Noah had the copy and emblem of it in the ark. In God, this Ark of blessedness, are all good things virtually to be found. Therefore Jacob, having God for his reward, could say, "I have enough"; or, as it is in the original, "I have all," Genesis 33:11. God is all marrow and fatness. He is such an exuberant reward as exceeds our very faith. If the Queen of Sheba's heart fainted within her to see all King Solomon's glory, what would it have done to have beheld the astonishing and magnificent reward which God bestows upon His favorites?
God is a suitable reward. The soul, being spiritual, must have something comparable and suitable to make it happy, and that is God. Light is no more suitable to the eye, nor melody to the ear, than God is to the soul.

He pours in spiritual blessings, Ephesians 1:3. He enriches it with grace, feasts it with His love, and crowns it with heavenly dignity.

God is a pleasant reward. He is the quintessence of delight, all beauty and love. To be feeding upon the thoughts of God is delicious. Psalm 104:34: "My meditation of Him shall be sweet." It is delightful to the bee to suck the flower; so, by holy musing, to suck out some of the sweetness in God carries a secret delight in it. To have a prospect of God only by faith is pleasant. 1 Peter 1:8: "In whom believing ye rejoice." Then what will the joy of vision be when we shall have a clear, intuitive sight of Him and be laid in the bosom of divine love! Is God so sweet a reward in affliction? 2 Corinthians 7:4: "I am exceedingly joyful in all our tribulation." Philip, Count of Hesse, said that in his confinement he had the divine consolation of the martyrs. Then what a delicious reward will God be in heaven! This may be better felt than expressed. The godly, entering upon their celestial reward, are said to enter into the joy of their Lord, Matthew 25:21. Oh, amazing! The saints enter into God's own joy. They have not only the joy which God bestows, but the joy which God enjoys.

God is a transcendent reward. The painter, going to take the picture of Helena, not being able to draw her beauty as in life, drew her face covered with a veil. So, when we speak of God's excellencies, we must draw a veil. He is so supereminent a reward that we cannot set Him forth in all His orience and magnificence. Put the whole world in balance with Him and it is as if you should weigh a feather with a mountain of gold. God has got the ascendant of all things. He is better than the world, better than the soul, better than heaven. He is the original cause of all good things. Nothing is sweet without Him. He perfumes and sanctifies our comforts. He turns the venison into a blessing.

God is an infinite reward. And, being infinite, these two things follow:

This reward cannot come to us by way of merit. Can we merit God? Can finite creatures merit an infinite reward?

God being an infinite reward, there can be no defect or scantiness in it. There is no want in that which is infinite. Some may ask, "Is God sufficient for every individual saint?" Yes. If the sun, which is but a finite creature, disperses its light to the universe, then much more God, who is infinite, distributes glory to the whole number of the elect. Every individual Christian has a membership in a community. As every person enjoys the whole sun to himself, so every believer possesses the whole God to himself. The Lord has land enough to give all His heirs. Throw a thousand buckets into the sea and there is water enough in the sea to fill them. Though there are millions of saints and angels, there is enough God to fill them. God is an infinite reward, and though He is continually giving out of His fullness to others, yet He has not the less. His glory is imparted, not impaired. It is a distribution without a diminution.

God is an honorable reward. Honor is the height of men's ambition. Aristotle calls it the greatest of blessings. Alas! Worldly honor is but a pleasing fancy. Honor has often a speedy burial; but to enjoy God is the head of honor. What greater dignity than to be taken up into communion with the God of glory, and to possess a kingdom with Him, bespangled with light, and seated above all the visible orbs?

A great heir, while in a foreign land, may be despised; but in his own country he is held in veneration. Here the people of God are as princes in a disguise, 1 John 3:1. But they shall have honor enough in heaven when they shall be clothed with white robes and sit with Christ upon His throne, Revelation 3:21.

God is an everlasting reward. Mortality is the disgrace of all earthly things. They are in their fruition surfeiting and in their duration dying. They are like that metal which glass is made of, which, when it shines brightest, is nearest melting. But God is an eternal reward. Eternity cannot be measured by years, jubilees, ages, nor the most slow motion of the eighth sphere. Eternity makes glory weighty. Psalm 48:14: "This God is our God for ever and ever." Oh, you saints of God, your praying and repenting are but for a while, but your reward is forever. As long as God is God, He will be rewarding you. Hosea 2:19: "I will betroth thee unto me forever." God marries Himself to His people, and this admits of no divorce. God's love for His elect is as unchangeable as His love for Christ. Psalm 73:26: "My portion forever." This portion cannot be spent because it is infinite, nor lost because it is eternal. We read of a river of pleasures at God's right hand, Psalm 36:8.

But, you may ask, may not this river be dried up?

No, for there is a fountain at the bottom. Psalm 36:9: "With Thee is the fountain of life."

QUESTION. But if this reward is so exceedingly great, will it not overwhelm us?

ANSWER. In the other world our faculties shall be

extended, and through the Mediator, Christ, we shall be made capable of receiving this reward. Put a plate of steel behind a glass and you may see your face in it. So, Christ's human nature being put as steel to the divine, God's glory will be seen and enjoyed by us. As there is no seeing the sun in the circle but in the beams, so, whatever of God is made visible to us will be through the golden beams of the Sun of Righteousness.

QUESTION. Where does the certainty of this reward appear?

ANSWER. God, who is the oracle of truth, has asserted it. A charter, legally confirmed under the Broad Seal, is unquestionable. The public faith of heaven is engaged to make good this reward. God's oath is laid at pledge, Psalm 58:11. Nay, God has not only pawned His truth, the most orient pearl of His crown, but He has given the anticipation and first fruits of this reward to His saints in joy and consolation, Galatians 5:22, which assures them of a harvest afterwards.

QUESTION. But when shall we be possessed of this reward?

ANSWER. The time is not long. Revelation 22:12: "Behold, I come quickly; and My reward is with Me." Sense and reason think it a long interval, but faith looks at the rewards as near. Through a perspective glass, the object which is at some distance seems near to the eye. So, when faith looks through the perspective glass of a promise, the reward seems near. As faith substantiates, so it anticipates things not seen; it makes them present, Ephesians 2:6.

QUESTION. But why is this reward at all deferred?
ANSWER 1. God does not see fit that we should yet
receive it. Our work is not done; we have not yet finished the faith. A day laborer does not receive his pay
till his work is done. Even Christ's reward was deferred
till He had completed His mediatorial work and said
upon the cross, "It is finished."
ANSWER 2. God defers the reward that we may live
by faith. We are taken with the reward, but God is
more taken with our faith. No grace honors God like
faith, Romans 4:20. God has given Himself to us by
promise. Faith trusts God's bond, and patience waits
for the payment.
ANSWER 3. God adjourns the reward a while to
sweeten it and make it more welcome to us when it
comes. After all our labors, watchings, and conflicts,
how comfortable will the reward be! Nay, the longer
the reward is deferred, it will be the greater. The
longest voyages have the largest returns.
If still it is asked, "When shall the time of this reward be?" I say, the righteous shall receive part of their
reward at death. No sooner is the soul out of the body
than it is present with the Lord, 2 Corinthians 5:8. And
the full coronation is at the resurrection when the soul
and body shall be united and perfected in glory.
Christians, do not faint in your voyage, though troublesome. You are within a few leagues of heaven. Your
salvation is now nearer than when you first believed,
Romans 13:11.
Several corollaries follow.

USE 1. OF INFORMATION.
BRANCH 1. Hence it is evident that it is lawful to

look to the future reward. God is our reward; is it not lawful to look to Him? Moses had an eye to the recompense of reward, Hebrews 11:26. What was this reward but God Himself? Verse 27: "As seeing Him who is invisible." Looking to the reward quickens us in religion. It is like the rod of myrtle in the traveler's hand which, it is said, revives his spirits and makes him walk without being weary. Who that is subject to fainting fits will not carry cordial water with him?

BRANCH 2. If God is such an exceedingly great reward, then it is not in vain to engage in His service. It was a slanderous speech, "Ye have said, It is vain to serve God," Malachi 3:14. The infinite Jehovah gives a reward that is as far beyond our thoughts as it is above our deserts. How apt are persons, through ignorance or mistake, to misjudge the ways of God! They think it will not be worth the cost to be religious. They speak evil of religion before they have tried it; as if one should condemn a meat before he has tasted it. Beside the gratuities which God gives in this life—provision, protection, and peace—there is a glorious reward shortly coming, Psalm 19:11. God Himself is the saints' dowry. God has a true monopoly. He has those riches which are nowhere else to be had, the riches of salvation. He is such a gold mine as no angel can find the bottom, the unsearchable riches of Christ, Ephesians 3:8. Is it vain, then, to serve God? A Christian's work is soon over, but not his reward. He has such a harvest coming as cannot be fully taken in. It will always be reaping time in heaven. How great is that reward which thoughts cannot measure nor time finish!

BRANCH 3. See the egregious folly of such as refuse God. Psalm 81:11: "Israel would have none of

Me." Is it usual to refuse rewards? If a man should have a vast sum of money offered to him and he should refuse it, his discretion would be called into question. God offers an incomprehensible reward to men, yet they refuse. They are like a magnet which refuses gold and pearl and draws rusty iron to it instead. Man, by his fall, lost his headpiece; he does not see where his interest lies. He flies from God as if he were afraid of salvation, and what does he refuse God for? The pleasures of the world; we may write upon them "temporary." These are like Noah's dove, which brought an olive branch in her mouth but quickly flew out of the ark. And to lose God for these perishables is an example of folly worse than that of Lysimachus, who, for a draft of water, lost his kingdom. We read in Scripture of two cups. Psalm 16:5: "The Lord is the portion of my cup." They who refuse this cup shall have another cup to drink of—Psalm 11:6: "Upon the wicked He shall rain snares, fire, and brimstone: this shall be the portion of the cup."

BRANCH 4. If God is such an immense reward, then see how little cause the saints have to fear death. Are men afraid to receive rewards? There is no way to live but by dying. Christians would be clothed with glory, but are loath to be unclothed. They pray, "Thy kingdom come," and when God is leading them there they are afraid to go. What makes us desirous of staying here? There is more in the world to wean us than to tempt us. Is it not a valley of tears? And do we weep to leave it? Are we not in a wilderness among fiery serpents? And are we loath to leave their company? Is there a better friend we can go to than God? Are there any sweeter smiles or softer embraces than His? Sure, those who know that when they die they go to receive their reward should neither be fond of life nor fearful of death. The pangs of death to believers are but the pangs of travail by which they are born into glory.

USE 2. OF EXHORTATION.

BRANCH 1. Believe this reward. Look not upon it as a Platonic idea or fancy. Sensualists question this reward because they do not see it. They may as well question the verity of their souls because, being spirits, they cannot be seen. Where should our faith rest but upon a divine testimony? We believe there are such places as Africa and America (though we have never seen them) because travelers who have been there affirm it. And shall we not believe the eternal recompenses when God Himself affirms them? The whole earth hangs upon the Word of God's power, and shall not our faith hang upon the Word of His truth? Let us not be skeptics in matters of such importance.

The Rabbis tell us the great dispute between Cain and Abel was about the future reward. Abel affirmed it; Cain denied it. The disbelief of this grand truth is the cause of the flagitiousness of the age. Immorality begins at infidelity, Hebrews 3:12. To mistrust a future reward is to question the Bible and to destroy a main article of our Creed: "Life everlasting." Such atheists as look upon God's promise but as a forged deed put God to swear against them, that they shall never enter into His rest, verse 18.

BRANCH 2. If God is such an exceeding great reward, let us endeavor that He may be *our* reward. In other things we love an ownership: "This house is mine, this lordship and manor is mine"; and why not

"This God is mine"? Pharaoh said to Moses and Aaron, "God sacrifice to your God." It was not "to my God." Leaving out one word in a will may spoil the will. Leaving out this word "my" is the loss of heaven. Psalm 67:6: "God, even our own God, shall bless us." He who can pronounce this shibboleth, "my God," is the happiest man alive.

QUESTION. How shall we know that God is our reward? There are four ways:

1. If God has given us the earnest of this reward. This earnest is His Spirit. Ephesians 1:13-14: "Ye were sealed with that Holy Spirit of promise, which is the earnest of our inheritance." Where God gives His Spirit for an earnest, there He gives Himself for a portion. Christ gave the purse to Judas, not His Spirit.

How shall we know we have God's Spirit?

The Spirit carries influence along with it. It consecrates the heart, making it a holy of holies. It sanctifies the fancy, causing it to mint holy thoughts. It sanctifies the will, strongly biasing it to good. As musk, lying among linen, perfumes it, so the Spirit of God in the soul perfumes it with sanctity.

But are not the unregenerate said to partake of the Holy Ghost?

They may have the common gifts of the Spirit, but not the special grace. They may have the enlightening of the Spirit, but not the anointing. They may have the Spirit move in them but not live in them. But to partake of the Holy Ghost aright is when the Spirit leaves lively impressions upon the heart. It softens, sublimates, and transforms it, writing a law of grace there, Hebrews 8:10. By this earnest we have a title to the reward.

2. If God is our reward, He has given us a hand to lay hold on Him. This hand is faith. Mark 9:24: "Lord, I believe." A weak faith justifies. As a weak hand can tie the knot in marriage, a weak faith can lay hold on a strong Christ. The nature of faith is assent joined with affiance, Acts 8:37 and 16:31. Faith makes God ours. Other graces make us *like* Christ, faith makes us one *with* Him. And this faith is known by its virtue. Said Cardan, "No precious stone but has some virtue latent in it." Precious faith has virtue in it; it quickens and ennobles; it puts worth into our services, Romans 16:26; it puts a difference between the "Abba, Father" of a saint and the "Ave, Mary" of a Papist.

3. We may know God is our reward by our choosing Him. Religion is not a matter of chance but of choice, Psalm 119:30. Have we weighed things in the balance, and, upon mature deliberation, made an election: "We will have God upon any terms"? Have we sat down and reckoned the cost? What religion *must* cost us—parting with our lusts—and what it *may* cost us—parting with our lives? Have we resolved, through the assistance of grace, to own Christ when the swords and staves are up? And to sail with Him not only in a pleasure boat but in a man-of-war? This choosing God speaks Him to be ours. Hypocrites profess God out of worldly design, not religious choice.

4. God is known to be our reward by the delight we take in Him, Psalm 37:4-8. How men please themselves with rich portions! What delight a bride takes in her jewels! Do we delight in God as our eternal portion? Indeed, He is a whole paradise of delight. All excellencies meet in God as the lines in a center. Is ours a genuine delight? Do we not only delight in God's blessings

but in God Himself? Is it a superior delight? Do we delight in God above other things? David had His crown-revenues to delight in, but his delight in God took place over all other delights. Psalm 43:4: "God, my exceeding glory," or, as it is in the original, "the gladness" or "cream of my joy." Can we delight in God when other delights are gone? Habakkuk 3:17-18: "Although the fig tree shall not blossom . . . yet I will rejoice in the Lord." When the flowers in a man's garden die, yet he can delight in his land and money. Thus a gracious soul, when the creature fades, can rejoice in the pearl of price. Paulinus, when they told him the Goths had sacked Nola and plundered him of all, lifted up his eyes to heaven and said, "Lord, Thou knowest where I have laid up my treasure." By this delighting in God we may undoubtedly know He is our reward.

QUESTION. What shall we do to get God to be our reward?

ANSWER. First, let us see our need of God. We are undone without Him. Do not lift up the crest of pride. Beware of the Laodicean temper, Revelation 3:17: "Thou sayest, I am rich and have need of nothing." God will never bestow Himself on those who see no want of Him.

Second, let us beg God to be our reward. It was Augustine's prayer, "Lord, give me Thyself." Psalm 17:14: "O do not put me off with common mercies; give me not my portion in this life." Be earnest suitors and God cannot find it in His heart to deny you. Prayer is the key of heaven which, being turned by the hand of faith, opens all God's treasures.

BRANCH 3. Live every day in the contemplation of this reward. Be in the altitudes. Think what God has prepared for those who love Him! Oh, that our thoughts could ascend! The higher the bird flies the sweeter it sings. Let us think how blessed they are who are possessed of their heritage. If one could but look a while through the chinks of heaven's door and see the beauty and bliss of Paradise, if he could but lay his ear to heaven and hear the ravishing music of those seraphic spirits and the anthems of praise which they sing, how would his soul be exhilarated and transported with joy!

Oh, Christians, meditate on this reward! Slight, transient thoughts do no good. They are like breath upon steel which is immediately off again. But let your thoughts dwell upon glory till your hearts are deeply affected. "What, Lord! Is there such an incomprehensible reward to be bestowed upon me? Shall these eyes of mine be blessed with transforming thoughts of Thee? Oh, the love of God to sinners!" Stand at this fire of meditation till your hearts begin to be warm. How would the reflection on this immense reward conquer temptation and behead those unruly lusts that have formerly conspired against us! "What! Is there a reward so sure, so sweet, so speedy? And shall I forfeit this by sin? Shall I, to please my appetite, lose my crown? Oh, all ye pleasure of sin, begone! Let me no more be deceived by your sugared lies. Wound me no more with your silver darts. Though stolen waters are sweet, yet the water of life is sweeter."

There is no stronger antidote to expel sin than the forethoughts of the heavenly remunerations. It was when Moses was long out of sight that Israel made an idol to worship, Exodus 32:1. So, when the future reward is long out of our mind, then we set up some idol

lust in our hearts when we begin to worship.
BRANCH 4. This may content God's people. Though they have but little oil in the cruse and their estates are almost boiled away to nothing, their reward is yet to come. Though your pension is small, your portion is large. If God is yours by deed of gift, this may rock your hearts quiet. God lets the wicked have their pay beforehand. Luke 6:24: "Ye have received your consolation." A wicked man will make his acquittance and write, "Received in full payment." But the saints' reward is in reversion—the robe and the ring are yet to come. May not this tune their hearts into contentment? Christian! What if God denies you a kid to make merry? If He says, "Son, all that I have is thine," Luke 15:31, is not this sufficient? Why do you complain of the world's emptiness when you have God's fullness? Is not God reward enough? Has a son any cause to complain that his father denies him a flower in the garden when he makes him heir to his estate?

The philosopher comforted himself with this, that though he had no music or vine trees, yet he had the household gods with him. So, Christian, though you do not have much of the world, yet you have God, and He is an inexhaustible treasure. It was strange, after God had told Abraham, "I am thy exceeding great reward," that Abraham should yet say, "Lord God, what wilt Thou give me seeing I go childless?" Genesis 15:2. Shall Abraham ask, "Lord, what wilt Thou give me?" when He had given Himself? Was Abraham troubled at the want of a child when he had a God? Was not God "better than ten sons"? Who *should* be content if not he who has God for his portion and heaven for his haven?

Let this exceedingly great reward stir up in us a

spirit of activity for God. Our head should study for
Him; our hands should work for Him; our feet should
run in the way of His commandments. Alas! How little
is all that we can do! Our work bears no proportion
with our reward. The thoughts of this reward should
make us rise off the bed of sloth and act with all our
might for God. It should add wings to our prayers and
weight to our alms. A slothful person stands in the
world for a cipher, and God writes down no ciphers in
the book of life. Let us abound in the work of the
Lord, 1 Corinthians 15:58. As aromatic trees sweat out
their precious oils, so should we sweat out our strength
and spirits for Christ.

Paul, knowing what a splendid reward was ahead,
brought all the more glory he could to God. 1
Corinthians 15:10: "I labored more abundantly than
they all." He outworked all the other apostles. Paul's
obedience did not move as slowly as the sun on the
dial, but as swiftly as the sun in the firmament. Did
Plato and Demosthenes undergo such Herculean
labors and studies, who had but the dim watch-light of
nature to see by, and did but fancy the pleasures of the
Elysian fields after this life? And shall not Christians
much more put forth all their vigor of spirit for God
when they are sure to be crowned, nay, God Himself
will be their crown?

BRANCH 5. If God is so great a reward, let such as
have an interest in Him be cheerful. God loves a sanguine complexion; cheerfulness credits religion. The
goodness of the conscience is seen in the gladness of
the countenance. Let the birds of Paradise sing for joy.
Shall a carnal man rejoice whose hopes lean on earthly
crutches, and shall not he rejoice whose treasure is laid

up in heaven? Be serious yet cheerful. As a dejected, melancholy temper makes one unfit for duty, especially that of praising God, so it disparages heaven. Will others think God is such a great reward when they see Christians hang the wing and go drooping in religion? It is a sin as well not to rejoice as not to repent.

OBJECTION. But how can I be cheerful? I am reduced to great straits.

ANSWER. Let God take away what He will from you, He will at last give you that which is better. As Pharaoh said, Genesis 45:20, "Regard not your stuff; for the good of all the land of Egypt is yours." Be not too much troubled at the diminution of these earthly things, for the good of all the land of heaven is yours. In the fields of Sicily there is a continual spring, and flowers are there all year long—an emblem of the Jerusalem above where flowers of joy are always growing. There you shall tread upon stars, be fellow commoners with angels, and have communion with the blessed Trinity. Let the saints, then, be glad in the Lord. In God are treasures that can never be emptied and pleasures that can never be ended.

BRANCH 6. If God is an exceedingly great reward, let such as have hope in Him long for possession. Though it should not be irksome to us to stay here to do service, yet we should have a holy longing till the portion comes into our hand. This is a temper becoming a Christian—content to live, desirous to die, Philippians 1:23-25. Does not the bride desire the day of espousals? Revelation 22:17. If we seriously considered our condition here—we are compassed with a body of sin; we cannot pray without wandering; we cannot believe without doubting—would not this make

us desire to have our pass, to be gone? Let us think
how happy those saints above are who are solacing
themselves in God. While we live far from court, they
are always beholding the smiling face of God. While we
drink wormwood, they swim in honey. While we are
perplexed between hope and fear, they know their
names are enrolled in the book of life. While we are
tossed upon the unquiet waves, they have gotten to the
haven. If we but knew what a reward God is, and what
the joy of our Lord means, we would need patience to
be content to stay here any longer.

BRANCH 7. Let such as have God for their exceedingly great reward be living organs of God's praise.
Psalm 118:28: "Thou art my God, and I will praise
Thee." Themistocles thought he was well requited by
the Grecians for his valor when they took such notice
of him in the Olympics, saying, "This is Themistocles."
God counts it requital enough for all His love when we
are grateful and present Him with our thank offering;
and well may we stand upon Mount Gerizim, blessing
and praising, if we consider the greatness of this reward. That we should be made heirs of God, and that
this surpassing reward is not a debt but a legacy, and
that, when many are passed by, the lot of free grace
should fall upon us—let this make us ascribe praise to
the Lord. It is called "the garment of praise" in Isaiah
61:3. The saints never look so comely as in this garment. Praise is the work of heaven; such as shall have
angels' reward should do angels' work. The word
"praise" comes from a Hebrew word that signifies to
shoot up. The godly should send up their praises as a
volley of shot toward heaven. Shall you live with God
and partake of His fullness in glory? Break forth into

doxologies and triumphs; long for that time when you shall join in concert with the angels, those choristers of heaven, in sounding forth hallelujahs to the King of glory. Such as are monuments of mercy should be patterns of thankfulness.

USE 3. OF CONSOLATION.

Will God Himself be His people's reward? This may be as an antidote to revive and comfort them:

1. In case of losses. They have lost their livings and promotions for conscience's sake, but as long as God lives their reward is not lost, Hebrews 10:34. Bernard said, "I cannot be poor as long as God is rich, for His riches are mine." Whatever we lose for God we shall find again in Him. In Mark 10:28 the disciples said, "We have left all and have followed Thee." Alas! What had they left? A few sorry boats and tackling! What were these to their reward? They parted with movable goods for the unchangeable God. All losses are made up in Him. We may be losers *for* God, but we shall not be losers *by* Him.

2. In case of persecution. The saints' reward will abundantly compensate for all their sufferings. Agrippa was laid in chains for Caius the latter. When he came later to the empire, he released Agrippa out of prison and gave him a chain of gold bigger than his iron chain. So God will infinitely remunerate those who suffer for Him. For their "waters of Marah" they shall have the wine of Paradise. The saints' sufferings are but for a while, 1 Peter 5:10, but their reward is forever. They are but a while in the winepress, but ever in the banqueting house. The Hebrew word for "glory" signifies a weight. The weight of glory should make af-

fliction light. The enjoying of God eternally will cause
Christians to forget all their sorrows. One beam of the
Sun of Righteousness will dry up their tears. After
trouble, peace; after labor, rest. Then God will be all in
all to His people—light to their eye, manna to their
taste, music to their ear, and joy to their heart. Oh,
then, let the saints be comforted in the midst of their
trials! Romans 8:18: "I reckon that the sufferings of this
present time are not worthy to be compared with the
glory which shall be revealed in us."

USE 4. OF TERROR TO THE WICKED.

Here is a Gorgon's head to frighten them. They
shall have a reward, but one vastly different from the
godly. The one shall be rewarded in the king's palace,
the other in prison. All the plagues in the Bible are
their reward. Proverbs 10:29: "Destruction shall be to
the workers of iniquity." God is their rewarder, but not
their reward. Romans 6:23: "The wages of sin is death."
They who did the devil's work will tremble to receive
their wages.

Zophar notably sets forth a wicked man's reward.
Job 20:7: "He shall perish forever like his own dung."
That is, he shall leave a stinking savor behind. Verse
16: "He shall suck the poison of asps." That is, the sin
which was sweet as honey in his mouth shall be as bitter as the gall of asps. Verse 26: "A fire not blown shall
consume him." That is, either a fire falling from
heaven shall consume him, as it did Korah; or by "a fire
not blown" may be meant a fire casually happening
among his goods and chattels shall consume him; or "a
fire not blown," that is, the fire of hell, not blown with
bellows, shall torture his soul. He shall be ever consum-

ing, never consumed. Verse 29: "This is the portion of a wicked man," and how tremendous is this! For every golden sand of mercy that runs out to a sinner, God puts a drop of wrath into His vial.